AMERICAN SYNDICALISM
THE I.W.W.

By

JOHN GRAHAM BROOKS

DA CAPO PRESS • NEW YORK • 1970

A Da Capo Press Reprint Edition

This Da Capo Press edition of *American Syndicalism: The I. W. W.* is an unabridged republi-
cation of the first edition published in New York
in 1913.

Library of Congress Catalog Card Number 78-107407

SBN 306-71887-1

Published by Da Capo Press
A Division of Plenum Publishing Corporation
227 West 17th Street, New York, N.Y. 10011
All Rights Reserved

Manufactured in the United States of America

AMERICAN SYNDICALISM

THE MACMILLAN COMPANY
NEW YORK · BOSTON · CHICAGO
DALLAS · SAN FRANCISCO

MACMILLAN & CO., LIMITED
LONDON · BOMBAY · CALCUTTA
MELBOURNE

THE MACMILLAN CO. OF CANADA, LTD.
TORONTO

AMERICAN SYNDICALISM

THE I. W. W.

BY

JOHN GRAHAM BROOKS

AUTHOR OF "AS OTHERS SEE US," "THE SOCIAL UNREST," ETC.

New York

THE MACMILLAN COMPANY

1913

PREFATORY NOTE

A considerable part of this volume was given as lectures at the University of California in 1911. For present purposes, the material has been recast and wholly rewritten.

The space given to the more general socialist movement and to the European origins of Syndicalism is justified on the ground that our tantalizing I. W. W. are not otherwise to be understood. Beyond Socialism, these represent the most revolutionary phases of social and economic revolt.

This combative, frontier character of the movement is so reflected in its literature and among its followers, that almost any statement one may make about syndicalist principles will meet direct denial. Between the higher and more theoretic syndicalists and the practical fighting members in the field of agitation, the differences in the interpretation of principles are radical to the point of confusion. This could not be otherwise in convulsive mass-action like that which characterizes syndicalist strategy.

CONTENTS

AMERICAN SYNDICALISM

I

THE SOCIALIST INVASION

UNTIL within some half dozen years, the sturdiest Americans were at most tepidly amused that any one should speak seriously of socialism. I have preserved an impatient letter from a very masterful financier, in which he asks a little querulously what good reason can be given for talking and writing "in this country" about a thing so unreal and freakish. He knew that some leading nations in Europe were at their wit's end to circumvent this propaganda. He thought the future very dark for some of those countries, especially for England. But what had all this to do with our own country? Did any one doubt the prosperity of the United States? Were not opportunities so ample that the whole world rushed in to seize them? He had examined the savings banks in New York City, "with their half million of depositors, mostly among poor people." Were there not four thousand millions in the Savings Banks of the Nation? He had at his finger tips the great army of stockholders in our railroads and leading corporations. Who could question that these beneficent agencies were distributing property to an ever widening proportion of our population? These were indeed "our democratic institutions." He believed that the coming census would prove that economic opportunity never was so great for the common man. It was upon observations like these that he based his protest. It was to him a criminal folly to keep these disturbing speculations alive.

I do not here put in question his views about the spread of property, but the main thought in this strong man's mind was that our American conditions so differed from those in Europe, that we were snug and secure from collectivist taints, if only this irresponsible prattle about socialism could be hushed up.

For quite thirty years, I have heard this view uttered with every variation of emphasis. Blind as it is, it had one excuse. From 1848, German socialists came here in such numbers as to give color to the statement that the mischief was merely an affair of disgruntled and whimpering foreigners. It pleased us to think of these unhappy strangers, fleeing from sombre tyrannies to a land so dazzling with freedom that the very excess of light caused them to blink and stumble. With good-natured tolerance, we humored and despised them. For some forty years they were the active center of such socialism as we knew.

All this has changed. No one can now examine with any care the socialist leadership as it appears in political and other activities, without seeing that we have to do with a movement that is in no proper sense "foreign." One of our most commanding figures in the railroad world says that the only practical issue now is to "stave socialism off as long as possible." He is convinced that the first chill of the shadow has fallen upon us. There is much reason to believe that socialism in its more revolutionary character is from now on to have its most fruitful field in the United States. The conditions and the mechanism through which it develops are in many ways more favorable here than in any country of Europe. Our prosperities, our higher wages, the mobility of the labor class, the immediate effect of our freer ways upon the incoming peasant all work to this end. Armies of these simple folk pass violently to the tense and unwonted excitements of city life or to industrial centers charged with hostilities between capital and labor. There is no saving transition between the habits and traditions which they bring and the new life to which they come. Of all that is deepest in these habits and traditions, our own ignorance is so elaborate and complete as to constitute a danger no less threatening. We have long sought comfort in thinking of our country as immune from really serious social agitations. German socialism used to be accounted for as "a reaction against the monarchy." English "landlord monopoly" was given as an explanation of the collectivist uprising in that country. But France is a republic and her land is largely in the hands of small farmers, yet socialists sit in her cabinet and a socialist has been Prime Minister. Denmark is a nation of small farmers who own most of the land and are not oppressed by their monarch, but there has developed there one of the most powerful socialist parties in Europe. In the North of Italy (as in the regions round about Mantua) there is a vigorous and growing socialism among agricultural workers quite as aggressive as any that the towns can show.

Thus socialism steadily wins its way underneath all these differences. Language, religion, forms of government set no barrier to its growth, because the causes of socialism underlie all these. The causes have their roots in the discovered excesses of a competitive system that fails to meet the minimum of equality which powerful sections in these communities now demand. In no part of the world have these excesses been more riotous than in the United States. Nowhere have they been brought more widely or more directly home to the masses than in this country. The magnitude of our area and of our economic resources have concealed and delayed the exposure. With the opening of the twentieth century the exposure has come.

After three decades of obscure and fitful struggle socialism becomes part and parcel of our political and social structure. It no longer stammers exclusively in a tongue half learned. It is at home in every American dialect. It no longer apologizes, it defies. Almost suddenly it wins a congressman, fifty mayors, and nearly a thousand elected officials.

As has happened in every known country where Socialism has grown strong, its first victories are followed by defeat. Pecuniary interests once alarmed, drop their differences and act together.

Many times this fusion has triumphed with boisterous self congratulation. For the most part the laughter has been premature. It soon turns out that the routed enemy has gathered again in larger numbers, more firmly entrenched and better equipped. In Milwaukee at the close of Mayor Seidel's first term, he and his socialist following are thrown out by the help of the Catholic Church and by the rapturous union of the two old parties which had fought each other for spoils since the Civil War. Socialism compels this fusion of frightened property interests into one grim phalanx bent upon its own safety. At the first threat of a common peril, the old banners—Republican or Democratic are forgotten. It is now property and privilege—the real forces underlying so much of our pretty political vaporing, that stand there like armored colleagues against the new enemy. Socialists are put to rout by this coalition though the socialist cause meantime has grown apace. The chuckling which echoed far and near over this "Milwaukee defeat" may later excite its own soberer reflections.

With wonted good nature, the public, unalarmed and unrebuked, accepts all these results. In accounting for the socialist capture of so large a city, the press insists that the revolt was not after all very "socialistic." It was mainly "only a protest," gathering to itself all manner of critical ill-humors that have little or nothing to do with the thing called socialism.

There is much truth in this, but also some dangerous reserves of error. In a visit to these "socially captured cities" I found not only in centers like Milwaukee and Butte, but in country towns, of which some of us never heard, that hundreds of the more thoughtful citizens had voted the socialist ticket. Many reasons were given me for this, but two of them have special interest. First, because the cynical corruption and decay of our party politics had reached a stage intolerable to disinterested and self-respecting men. On its economic side, the pinching cost of living had stung these discontents into sharper expression. In larger and in smaller towns, I asked teachers, professional and business men, small shopkeepers and clergymen, why they had cast off allegiance to the Republican or Democratic party. A teacher active in the socialist propaganda gave this answer, which stands fairly enough for many others. "I stuck to the Republican Party for years after I knew it was affiliated with interests which made anything like honest government impossible in this city. Twice I voted for Democrats who, after some moral sputtering, fell down abjectly under machine influence. Once more I tried my old party, until I saw it had just rotted out. I'm not going to be fooled by this socialism. I see it promises a good many things it never can deliver, but I shall stick to it. I shall give it what money and time I can afford, just as long as it shows its present spirit."

When I asked what he meant by this socialist "spirit," he said: "I mean its political disinterestedness. It probably uses a lot of big words it doesn't half understand, but it has none of the palaver of cant and humbug that characterized Republicans and Democrats alike when they addressed the working class. These Socialists really do act as unselfishly as they talk and no big interests are behind them." He then told me the story of unpaid drudgery which hundreds of hard working men and women gave on Sundays and the hours before and after their long working days. It was the tale I had heard or the thing

I had seen in several other cities under socialist control. It is a story one may hear in every part of the United States.

In another city, barely escaping socialist majorities, a teacher old enough to remember the Civil War gave me the same record of experience. "I haven't had a political thrill, except of disgust, since those great days of my youth. Two bright boys in my Civics class began to bring me accounts of what local socialists were doing. I had read three or four socialist books of the better sort, but thought of them as stimulating and harmless Utopias. I then set to work on the local programs. I was surprised to find many of my old pupils and teachers consecrated to the movement, though many of them held positions which kept them silent. It has brought to me in my closing years the great emotions of 1860. I had come to believe that concentrating wealth had so fastened upon our political life as to lead us straight toward disaster. We may go there still, but this Socialism has restored my hope. It has made me believe there are moral resources in the community and intellectual capacities among common people which will save us, *if we are sane enough to recognize them and work with them.*"

I have emphasized these final words, because they hold a lesson that we must learn if we are capable of learning anything.. Later in this study the lesson will be taken up when further proofs of its significance can be given. It is very important at this point that the reader avoid the error of thinking these two illustrations are merely interesting exceptions. They are selected from a mass of testimony with the same significance, because they express the rebellious attitude with concreteness and lucidity. I found men and women teachers settled in their determinations to resign their positions in order to take active part in socialist work. In no case were these persons failures in their calling. An instructor of natural science in a high school said, "I am only waiting for an opening in the socialist ranks where I can be fairly certain of doing the kind of work that I think would count for the cause." He was prepared to take all the chances in earning a living. He found at every teachers' gathering more and more willing listeners and more readers of socialist literature.

Interfused as opinion and hope, these instances stand for a new faith and a new purpose held by two or three millions of our fellow citizens. If the ability and willingness to sacrifice oneself for an ideal are hopeful qualities, this rapidly growing body must be counted among our moral assets. If, in whole or in part, it is to be opposed, for that very reason it should be understood. Every attempt merely to outlaw it, to vilify or browbeat it, will prove the friendliest service its opponents can render to a cause they fear.[1] There is at the present moment in our midst no more dangerous obtuseness than that which constituted authority has been displaying from San Diego to

[1] The judicial part in the trial of Ettor, Giovannitti and Caruso which has just closed at Salem is an auspicious exception. If one could hope that the temper of the presiding judge in this instance would generally prevail throughout the country, the greater safety of every true social interest would be more secure.

Massachusetts towns. If it is the express object to multiply the agitators' power over labor, not twice or thrice but twenty times, it is easily done. Let an irritated citizenship itself play the anarchist, as in San Diego and in several Eastern communities; let it act in heat and with suspicious disregard for justice and at once a hundred new avenues of influence are opened to men like Ettor and Giovannitti. If they had gone to the electric chair, the incensed imagination of millions of workingmen and women would have crowned them martyrs. Solemn hours would have been set apart to do them honor and the place of their burial would have been a shrine. Even now, as they leave jail, audiences that no hall can hold will greet them rapturously in every industrial center of the United States. It matters little what they say; the sympathy that has been created in their favor supplies all deficiencies. Their lightest word has significance and carrying power that make the jail the shortest, quickest way to influence. A lawyer, himself doubting the justice of their jailing, tells me, "But severity might have worked best, as it did in hanging the Chicago anarchists in '87. There was little enough justice there, but the thing worked. You haven't heard of anarchists in that town since." Even if there were truth in this risky analogy, it is very fatal not to recognize the changes since 1887. Labor has many avenues of expression and influence now which it did not then possess. It has literary organs constantly read by at least four million of men and women. It has its first strategic hold upon our political life. It has a new and deepened sense of solidarity that strengthens month by month as it awakens to the nature of its task. It is an awakening immeasurably stimulated by critical and intensive studies that have become the best stock in trade for a dozen magazines and weeklies of the highest class. These disclosures of things sick and sickening among capitalistic disorders pour their steady current into every socialistic sheet. One of them has it, "We Socialists could discredit the present business and political system if we did nothing but re-edit and popularize what the big magazines are saying. They get a lot of better stuff than we can get."

The fateful note in the Lawrence strike was not in that distracted city. It was in the impression made upon almost every outside investigator. It was in the throb of fellow feeling, not for manager or for stockholder, but for strikers deprived of organization. In more than eighty articles in every variety of publication, from the *Atlantic Monthly* to the great dailies, this sympathy appeared. To my certain knowledge three persons with large possessions stood ready to help these strikers, if the case had gone too far against them.

I am not here defending this sympathy. I do not pass upon it as fair or even intelligent, I point to it solely as a *fact:* a fact very momentous because it has become an increasing part of labor's awakening and entry into politics.

All this has brought a new atmosphere with changed perspective, both in its lights and shadows. It is an atmosphere extremely favorable to the growth of socialism. The fear of the word is obviously passing.

There is a new hospitality to open and fearless discussion of its proposals. A growing number of editors, legislators, scholars, economists, sympathize with the propaganda to the extent, that they welcome and encourage its discussion. As for the "working classes," in centers of industry, as well as in newer agricultural communities of the West, conditions are such that the socialist vote may at any moment record itself in such force as to disturb profoundly our present party politics. We have now to count upon this as something irreducible. We shall neither stop it nor lessen its pace. Our impending question is one of learning so to adjust ourselves to the new fact that some real part is left us in shaping and guiding these new democratic urgencies toward stability rather than toward confusion and disorder.

II

THE MORE IMMEDIATE DANGER

In the hope of making more intelligible the general purpose of this study, I wish to connect it with experiences out of which an earlier volume grew—*The Social Unrest.* The book was at best only the A. B. C. of some economic disorders observable at the time. As in a primer, I tried to interpret those features of the trade union struggle, as it met on one side the resistance of the employer and upon the other an already invading socialism. It seemed to me then, as it seems today, that socialism has no such personal friend as the capitalist possessing power and inclination to crush labor organization. There are other and deeper causes of socialism over which we have little control, but in our relation to labor organization, we can exercise choice and conscious direction. Not all the bulky offences of trade union aggression should obscure the fact that these organizations are among the educational and conservative forces of our time. The trade union expressly recognizes the wage system and tries always, however awkwardly, to make terms with it. Just as expressly, socialism aims to destroy that system as part and parcel of the one "iniquitous despoiler," capitalism; i. e., our present methods of doing business.

Even in theory, if capital once convinces labor that its trade union is futile; that it can have no organic and recognized part with capitalist management, then

labor, if it have a gleam of intelligence, will look elsewhere for succor. It will say, "The capitalist refuses
to play fair with us. Real power in the business world
has become organic. Its great achievements now come
through organization. Knowing this and glorying
in it, capital either fights us or palavers. It fights or
it seeks diverting substitutes,—anything to prevent
that collective efficiency among us which it finds indispensable for itself."

My appeal is not, however, to theory, but to such fact
and open illustration as appear in pages that follow.

Before the sullen reactions of the Homestead Strike
in Pittsburg had ceased, I asked a man of real power
in those great industries, if it were true that he and
his friends had determined to wipe out trade union
organization. "Yes," he said, "that is our purpose.
They seem to exist only to make trouble and we are
done with them." Without excitement or bragga-
docio, he explained to me how this could be done and
would be done. "They bother the life out of us,"
he added. "They keep men at work we do not want;
prevent or try to prevent our turning off those for
whom we have no further use. They level things
toward the meanest worker. We have got on with
them only because we were forced to it. They everywhere check product. We are now going to control
our own business, and we are going to do it entirely." [1]

---

[1] This employer, like others, did not of course object to a "good
trade union"—one that would in no way interfere. But the employer
cannot be allowed to define "goodness" in a trade union any more
than we can allow labor to define it. The definition above them both
is that which public welfare finds workably just and fair for social
security.

I knew that in general and in detail, there was a good deal of truth in what this gentlemen said, but I left Pittsburg wondering what the American people would say, and especially what they would *continue* to say about this question. Quite incontestable is it that to most employers trade unions are a nuisance. But the employer's point of view is neither exclusive nor final. There is also the point of view of twenty-two or -three millions of wage earners. More important still is a point of view above them both; namely, that of the general public. The momentous event in our country is that at last the public is becoming aware of its right and its power as a collective whole. It will alas, be long in learning a wise and temperate use of its power. Because of its ignorance and much blundering, it will frighten many investors; discourage many enterprises; let loose upon us a pest of self-seeking politicians, but none of these unavoidable abuses will stop the growing assertion of public authority over the organized forces at war with each other in the ever widening field of competition. People have learned that if trade unions have bothered capital, so has capital bothered the public. Capitalistic organizations have annoyed the public in ways that are different, but so gravely have they threatened the community, that a large part of governmental energies, federal, state and city, is now devoted to a very desperate struggle with these incorporated forces. We are trying to control tendencies in them that are seen to be anti-social. Most people who retain their sanity, see that these interknitted powers neither can be nor ought to be crushed. That in the common interest, we must at least try to "regulate" them, is now admitted. This implies the necessity of organization. It also implies its justification. But why should street car systems, express companies, telegraph and mining corporations require organization, while the wage labor connected with them is deprived of it? Capital asks for organization because an unchecked competition raises plain havoc with its undertakings. Organization brings these pillaging disorders under conscious control which helps to steady and maintain price standards. But what of labor at the bottom? Is it less mercilessly beset by competition than is the employer?

With its mobility, with its facilities and habits of moving from place to place, and, above all, with the inpouring of multitudinous immigrants, is it to be held for an instant that labor stands in less urgent need of organization than capital? I have just put this question to an employer tormented by a strike over this very issue. He admits that "in theory perhaps" his men should have what he has and must have, organization. But "practically," he adds, "it is impossible. The men will misuse it. There will be constant and intolerable interference with our management."

Yes, there would be interference, precisely as society had been forced, in its own defense, to interfere with organized capital. We had a century of interference to create the whole structure of factory legislation, and now again begins another struggle to devise the agencies of regulating lawless propensities in the "trusts." There is not an aspect of our social policy that does not assume the fact and the necessity

of capitalistic organization and also that it is to be
"interfered" with by systematized control. It is the
very pick of our overlords who now tell us why regulation is inevitable.

The overlord in Pittsburg nearly twenty years ago,
said that capital had to be organized on such a scale,
that it was extremely open and sensitive to disturbances of all sorts and the trade union disturbance
was one that they could control with more safety and
more easily than any other. The statement is exact.
Capital in that neighborhood had power enough to
deny organization to labor. Troublesome workmen
could be quietly dropped. The energetic and skilled
could be paid above the trade union scale. It was all
so easy, if you had the power.

It was very ominous to the mere student to be told
so convincingly that this was the age of organization;
that all our towering prosperities depended upon it,
but that the wage man and woman, so far as possible,
should be excluded from it. For is it not also an age
of the common school; of contagious enlightenment
through the press; of rapidly multiplying agencies
of very definite labor agitation? Is it not the age when
Socialism appears, not as a cloud no larger than a
man's hand on the horizon, but in gathering hosts
like that of an army with banners?

In the face of all this, what must be the result of
this amazing attitude? "I, the capitalist, cannot
live without organization: without conceded privileges
from Government, State, or City; but you, swarming
and competing legions of labor, shall not have it.
You are so many, you are so ignorant, you are so

easily fooled by agitators. Though in theory you ought to have it, in practice we cannot trust you with its use." Leaving Pittsburg, I wondered what labor would continue to say of this and also what would be the final judgment of the general public. On the train I wrote out, as best I could, some fumbling answers to these questions. Who and what are they who receive wages that they should be excluded and set apart as unworthy to share in this indispensable form of association that is such a tower of strength to those who are already strong? Was it in the least likely that the mass of wage earners, sore under this treatment, would not resent it? If so, what shapes would this resentment assume? With popular agencies of agitation so far developed; with socialism already so vigorous in its rivalry with the unions, the case seemed clear. Capital could gain no victory over labor association that left its pang of felt injustice, without throwing the door wider still to socialism. In what appeared later in *The Social Unrest*, I wrote:

"It is not probable that employers can destroy unionism in the United States. Adroit and desperate attempts will, however, be made, if we mean by unionism the aggressive fact of vigorous and determined organizations.

"If capital should prove too strong in this struggle, the result is easy to predict. The employers have only to convince organized labor that it cannot hold its own against the capitalist manager, and the whole energy that now goes to the union will turn to an aggressive political socialism. It will not be the harmless sympathy with increased city and state functions which trade unions already feel; it will become a turbulent political force bent upon using every weapon of taxation against the rich."

"Those who represent the interests of capital must make the choice. With magnificent energy they have created an industrial organization that no other nation now matches. Will they use some fair portion of this strength *to complete this principle of organization so that it includes those who help them do their work?* or will they, in the fighting spirit of competition under which they were bred, insist upon an unrestrained and unmodified mastery?"

There are plenty of other causes for the rise of social unrest besides this defeat of effective labor organization, but in this country socialism owes an immense debt of gratitude to every capitalist who rejoices over the undoing of labor unions.

Some years later, I twice spent a week in Pittsburg. Though incomparably better at the top than twenty other roaring centers of industry, it was not worse at the bottom except in volume and intensity. As nowhere else, one could mark the massed energies of wealth-production at the point of utmost achievement. The top of the pyramid was in quite dazzling light. Priceless art collections open to the public, noble music, heaps of best books, and such higher schools as the country had not seen. But lower down upon the pyramid, the light turned into shadow; lower still, it grew black as pitch. Here in choking tenements was the forgotten city. Here were the legions that worked twelve hours in the day, and even Sundays. Here was the chaos of low and uncertain pay. Here was every incalculable shape that insecurity could take, all the horrors of maiming and unnatural death. On this great army of the forgotten rested the pyramid with its glistening cap.

But this was "great industry" in America. It was Pittsburg, only in heightened pace and concentration. For this reason came the ghastly "Survey" of that city. It directed public attention from the shining top to the broad base. After the main body of this wholly admirable investigation had been published, I found an ironmaster in the city who had read it. He was about half angry. He pointed out to me "mistakes," but in their relation to the whole disclosure these "mistakes" were so trivial as to excite laughter. "Yes," he said, "it is in the main true, but it makes a Pittsburger mad to have his own town picked out and held up as if it were the only sinner. In our business we are no worse than the rest of the world, and in many respects far better." Every one of us who is properly human will respond to this local patriotism. The "Survey" only shows us what an unfolding there would have been if investigators had done for the country as a whole what they did for Pittsburg. Restricted as it is, the popularized education based upon that study is beyond price.

Bits from the income of one great capitalist were used to pry off the lid of things subterranean, and let the public study what went on there. Owners, managers, and stockholders were compelled to see probably for the first time, what was really happening beneath the pyramid, under the shadow of which they lived. Clear as flame in a dark night, one fact stood out. Here was a business, touching and enveloping the life of the nation. Woodrow Wilson was just then saying in a public speech, "Business is no longer in any sense a private matter." "Society is the senior partner in all business." If this is tr ie, or half true, of "all business," what is to be said of this Colossus whose products are riveted into the whole material fabric of our existence? Through all the vast enginery, the phalanxes of labor passed, but at a pace and strain which burned out the vitality of average men in half life's working time.

Is this no business of the public? Who is to pay the bill for all the wreckage which such overpaced industries throw back upon the community? We do not forget that when managers themselves looked through the lid they, too, were startled into belated action. Quite magnificently have they set to work to standardize the human side of their industry; to deal with the living factor as cunningly as with steel beams and finance. This honorable step should have its recognition, but it is a beginning only, and the slowly waking public will continue to observe; to reflect and hold the managers to account.

It will press, too, that other question: Are the giants alone to have organization? If not, what follows?

Two years ago, I found in a Pittsburg suburb the first sure sign of Syndicalism that I had seen in the United States since its abrupt formation out of that portentous strike of Colorado miners in 1903–4. It was a strike in which the lawlessness of labor was matched and outmatched by the lawlessness of capital. The fruits of it were Syndicalism, or, as here named, the "Industrial Workers of the World." Belted and armed, it now enters the arena of discontent. For several weeks in 1911, I watched it in a half dozen cities on the Pacific coast.

The I. W. W. taps labor strata not only lower than those of the trade union, but still lower than those from which Socialism generally gets recruits. It appeals to youth, to the most detached and irresponsible, to those free to follow a life of adventure. It appeals to those who rebel at the discipline of the trade union. It easily becomes a brother to the tramp and the outcast. Nor is there one of these traits that is not a source of temporary strength from its own point of view—that of rousing and educating discontent, of hectoring and obstructing the solidities of capitalism. Every difference which a heterogeneous and unassimilated immigration means for the United States will advantage the I. W. W. We have consented to and encouraged the conditions out of which these *frondeurs* come. They are now integrally a part of us. Abuse and lawless rigors among good citizens will enrich both their material and emotional resources. As with the trade union and our more ripened socialism, this new and more refractory contingent must be understood. In spite of deliriums, it too holds its heart of truth. If it brings the plague, it also brings suggestion. For the classes more safely lodged, they are hints rather in the form of news that we ought to know; news like that which a scout brings in, untested, but with forewarnings that the wise do not ignore. We shall safely exclude no man on the firing line of social change.

If, in these grave concerns, we are to create a saving statesmanship it must have first of all the courage of open-mindedness, willing to listen even to I. W. Ws.: to know their leaders: yes, even to work with them rather than contemptuously and excludingly to work against them.

Local, legal and other authorities, during the last two years in the United States, have done more for the growth of this revolutionary group, shading into anarchy, than it has done for itself. This assistance has been rendered because the most important thing in the I. W. W. was misconceived by frightened property owners and by the officials who represented them. Social authorities on the Pacific coast insisted that the whole I. W. W. "bunch" was composed of "bums," and on that theory used the legal machinery in their control to harry them out of town. If the "Great Bad" is in "mixing things that do not belong together," this attitude accurately defines the Great Bad.

The I. W. W. movement is strictly a revolutionary uprising against that part of the present order which is known as capitalism. Its ground-swell is felt in many very different types of nationality. Like every revolution, it attracts the most unselfish and courageous, together with the self-seeking and the semi-criminal. Garibaldi's famous "Thousand" had in it as large a percentage of this latter class as the I. W. W. at its worst. The King of Naples tried to treat Garibaldi's followers like "bums." It proved a most damaging error, because these revolutionists began to excite powerful sympathy. It was a sympathy that soon passed into political action, as many of our own great strikes pass into politics, forcing employers to yield to a new and hated influence. As the revolt of labor increases, popular sympathy acts through politicians whom, if they are against us, we call "demagogues."

This is the landmark we have now reached. So many people have come to sympathize with the socialistic ideals that these disturbances can no longer be kept out of politics. It is a sympathy of such strength, that even politicians of high character will use it. A Public Service Corporation which has not now learned this lesson cannot even make the bluff that its managers are really practical men. No one can claim that distinction who ignores the most obdurate facts that enter into this kind of strike.

Yet all this is on the surface of our problem. What concerns us far more is the character and justification of this new popular sympathy with those in revolt. If the Boston Elevated Railroad in its strike of 1912, is forced to do finally about everything that it at first stoutly and rather contemptuously said it could not do, our interest is to know about the forces that brought about the change. If greater events like the English "Taff-Vail Decision" and the "Osborn Judgment" have finally to be utterly remodeled because a new political reckoning has to be made, we want also to know what meaning there is in this insistance that the most solemnly sanctioned laws must be changed; that labor shall retain rights and privileges that courts would deny, If the public, once instructed, will not stand it to see men discharged because they join a trade union, or because I. W. W. agitators are treated as "bums," it must suggest at least this,— that the deeper cause these agitators have at heart is misconceived by those who think such summary methods either wise or "practical." That these misunderstandings are now our most immediate danger seems to the writer so clear that some space must be given to justify this opinion.

Let us first note however, a change in the common atmosphere of industrial disturbance; the wider sweep of the world's sympathy with those about the base of the pyramid. We shall not otherwise see the meaning of the newer movement which is the special purpose of this study.

III

THE ENLARGEMENT OF THE PROBLEM

As something distinct from Socialism and from trade unionism, Syndicalism is now set down as a "World Movement." The claim is made that it has differentiated a revolutionary force of its own, sure to supersede the niggardly ways of ordinary labor organization, on the one side, and an entangled political Socialism on the other.

At the Lawrence strike, I saw a newcomer so fresh from the Old World, that he tripped awkwardly in almost every English sentence. But he was aglow with beneficence. He said he had been in eight different countries. "Always it is the same. Everywhere it is the one home. I had only to smile and say a little word—'Comrade.' At once something happens. I get quick my smile back and such great welcome. With 'Comrade' and no money, I could see all the world and learn all things."

There is neither measurement nor appreciation of this movement apart from the spirit revealed in this simple incident. Year by year each isolated group gets new strength and confidence from the thrill of its wider brotherhood. Scarcely a week passes that some electric event does not furnish proof of these tidal sympathies.

Among a dozen recent occurrences of our own is that at San Diego, California. Those of social and business importance, those in public office suddenly note increasing bands of I. W. W. orators about the streets. For practical reasons (like density of traffic) most towns set apart certain spaces on which public speaking is prohibited. Sometimes in ignorance and sometimes in defiance "to test free speech" the orators were found haranguing crowds upon these forbidden spots. Often this restricting ordinance had been forgotten—religious and political addresses being freely given on these interdicted areas. These promoters of the I. W. W. act like acid on parchment; the dimmed legal traceries flash out distinct as if written an hour ago. No I. W. W. shall now speak on these reserves, nor shall he speak anywhere else. In the heat and confusion, all the demarcations are lost and citizens proud of their behavior become more lawless than their invaders. The noise was such as to give unenviable notoriety to this town "with the best climate in the world." Just now it is aflame with speculative hopes based upon the early opening of the Panama water way. Property really frightened is almost certain to be cruel, and therefore to be shortsighted. Those socially ascendant in San Diego "went to it" with a high hand. There were almost barbaric cruelties, but there was more shortsightedness. They imagined themselves like Little Falls and Lawrence officials dealing only with their own community. "Surely in San Diego we can manage our own affairs and in our own way." From one of them, I heard the familiar expression, "But damnation! It's nobody's business outside this town." This remonstrance was caused by criticism in papers further up the state.

Criticism already rife in eastern papers was naturally answered with contempt. A few days later the surprise came. A report on local behavior had been ordered by the Governor of the State. It was published with maddening strictures on the methods of these same protectors of San Diego. The report was met with hot denials by local patriots. Then, armed with the authority of the State, the State's attorney appears upon the scene, and the "business of the town becomes the business of the State."

This same swift enlargement of the scene came to Lawrence, Massachusetts. There, too, it seemed at first a little matter only of local concern. To cut such a wage scale as Commissioner Neil's Report has now made clear, to cut it because fifty-four hours took the place of fifty-six; to cut it with so little regard for those affected, that no sort of adequate warning or explanation was given, shows how sure of itself the mill ownership felt. There was ground for this assurance. Conditions in Lawrence were no worse than in other mill towns, but ownership there had shown one doubtful superiority. It could hold organized labor effectually at bay. It could have for itself all that organization gives, but refuse it to labor. It could have generations of paternal tariff-coddling from Government to protect its product, at the same time that unprotected and competing labor was at its disposal. These were advantages that beget confidence; a kind of confidence that easily breeds arbitrary habits of mind. Thus the jar with its rude provoking came to Lawrence, as it came to San Diego. A lawyer said to me, "We are trying up here to mind our own business. I wouldn't mind a bit if the rest of the world did the same." He thought a vigorous purge that should clean his city from the nausea of sociologists would be a good beginning. They were doubtless a nuisance, these sociologists, but they, too, were a sign of something serious. Their irritating curiosity was only a bit of writing on the wall. The State also came as at San Diego, then the general Government looked in upon the mill town. Men came, equipped by long experience for their work. They "stayed upon the job." Pitiless and uncolored, the facts concerning wages had to come out. Employers under criticism behave like the rest of us. They put the best foot forward, call attention to the highest wages, direct the visitor to best conditions, precisely, as upon the other side, labor points to every haggard fact upon the scene; wretched housing, indecencies and abuse of foremen; petty personal discriminations, and every item of lowest and most uncertain labor income.

From socialist papers reporting the Lawrence strike, I cut for weeks their assertions about the wage scale. Their understatement was much like the overstatement of the management, even further from the truth. But now between these two exaggerations, the agents of the Government, in twenty thousand classified cases, came to state the facts with neither fear nor bias. This is "political interference," most cordially detested by business that thinks itself a private affair. But this "interference" has come to stay. Its growth is continuous in every country. It was long ago said of a religious movement, "It is like a naked sword, its hilt in Rome and its point

everywhere." Government interference is more and
more everywhere. We in the United States are very
laggard among the nations, but not a month passes
in which the sword's tip will not show itself in some
new center of conflict. *It is nothing in the world but
the groping insistence that the public is justly concerned
in these disturbances.* The sword's point is the public
point of view. In the hand of President Cleveland,
it had a long thrust in the case of the Pullman strike.
It was used by Roosevelt in the Anthracite Coal
Commission. It is now a fixed and permanent policy.

Senators and representatives appeared at Lawrence.
Rumor had it that Congressional investigations were
at hand with purposes to probe deeper than the strike.
And so this mill city rouses to the fact that her distress was neither local nor private. Like many another industrial center in recent years, she was an
object lesson of industrial maladjustment. Of this
maladjustment the nation is becoming conscious and
so it, too, plays the sociologist. Very slowly and with
much obstinacy, we are learning the great lesson that
neither the town nor the state nor the nation can
any longer act as if it were sufficient unto itself.

A plaintive Egyptian Pasha has just told us that
Turkey could have conquered Italy "if left alone."
"We owe our defeat," he says, "to Egypt's *neutrality*."
Together the nations had made Egypt "neutral" and
therefore Turkey could not use it as a highway for
troops, any more than Italy could strike Turkey by
closing the Dardanelles. This water way, too, was
neutralized—set apart by world agreement as a kind
of consecrated space which lesser units should respect.

For the first time, town after town, like Lawrence, Pittsburg and Little Falls learns with disgust, like the Turks, that it must act with reference to the enveloping life of which it is an integral and living part. Good citizens must not begin by themselves playing the anarchist. In the last year several communities have been robustly acting the anarchist rôle.

The most fundamental of all anarchies is the practical contempt for laws of our own making. Yet several of these centers have been under provocation so acute as to excite sympathetic understanding. In other Western towns, I saw I. W. W. behavior of so galling a nature, that no community known to me in the United States would have borne itself with dignity or perfect law-abidingness.

There is a line in Virgil which runs:

> If I cannot bend the powers above,
> I will rouse Hell.

The more bumptious of those raiding these towns had not even called upon the "powers above." They were very open in their declaration that "to raise hell" was one of their hearts' desires. It is true, that friends of theirs had been roughly and illegally handled. This was their excuse. The authorities said they feared trouble and for this reason acted as those who deal with a "situation rather than with a theory."

A social conflict has arisen among us between a "situation" and a "theory." Whatever our accepted "law and order" may mean, it is challenged by the socialist movement as a whole and very sharply challenged by a growing revolutionary section known as the "Industrial Workers of the World." They are not in the least disturbed that we name them "outlaws." If a half of what they say of our present society is true, the "outlaw" is the one heroic figure in our midst.

At the heart of the movement is an impulse and a motive which no one with open mind can really see without respect. The hectoring crudities of the movement are so in evidence, as to blot out what is best in an idealism which we should not lose. To forget that the movement has its idealism is not only to mistake it as a whole, but very wretchedly to bungle in our practical relations with it. Thus far I. W. W. victories have been largely won by the blunders of their enemies. This will continue until we know better what socialism in general really means and why a more giddy and harassing form of it now appears.

If it could become, once for all, clear to us what this means, it would save us from immeasurable ills. The government has taken no one of its ungainly steps in "interference" which was not forced upon it by the vague but importunate pressure of a changing public opinion. No politician has a feather's weight of influence in these interferences, beyond what the atmospheric pressure of this general opinion gives him. The scurviest demagogue can only take advantage of it.

Beginning with transportation; then with larger businesses in closest affiliation with these main arteries of traffic, the public has come to feel that these are *social* as well as private affairs. Above all, it has come to feel that they are no longer to be kept as the secret speculative tools of finance.

When Woodrow Wilson said that these were public rather than private, he was merely interpreting the growing collective opinion in this country. Until the more masterful holders of these centers of economic power recognize this and enter with some heartiness into more sympathetic coöperation with the new and altered opinion, both political and industrial friction will increase.

Against the spirit of secrecy and absolutism in this more powerful business management, the protest rises. Its warning comes from all those who would "regulate" these forces. It comes from collectivists, from socialists of every shade, and now, with shrill and mocking challenge, from a new "Order" of the I. W. W. It is a dangerous form of dullness merely to sniff at this latest note of protest. It is a part of something far greater than itself. Roughly, the word socialism stands for this larger thing, but especially about the spirit of this movement, foggy misconceptions still cling. A further appeal must be made to the reader's patience in a brief attempt to illustrate what seem to the writer some errors in interpreting the spirit and motive of the socialist protest and still more in all attempts to understand the I. W. W.

IV

THE PLAGUE OF MISCONCEPTIONS

(I)

WITH cynical hilarity a business friend has just read to me a proposal by Mr. Debs to raise at once "$500,000 for the approaching socialist campaign." "There you have it, like a staged farce. The starved millions, living on the margin of want, are to paint the country red with two million votes for Debs and Seidel. Not a nickel from the big interests, no blackmailing of corporations, but the whole half million subscribed by the starving, downtrodden working class." "And this," he adds, "is but an item. They pour thousands of dollars into Lawrence and a dozen other struck towns at the same time. They have just been buncoed out of a quarter of a million to free the McNamaras. They are paying for costly conventions, hundreds of lectures, and a very expensive press. Doesn't such penury wring the heart?"

In this sportive mood he filled in other features of the comedy, ending with that annihilating phrase— "They must be destitute of humor."

This gentleman had been telling a great deal of truth, but by no means all of it or the most important part of it. These objects of his lampooning are raising far larger funds than he knew. They are doing it all over the world, in countries where the purchasing

33

power of the year's income is far lower than in the
United States. They have for many years been doing
it on a scale which most well-to-do people would consider insane or criminal. The propertied classes very
generally shuffle and kick at ordinary taxes, but with
voluntary devotion millions of working men and
women bring hard earned money to support an idea.
They are not doing this in spurts of enthusiasm,
but with tireless persistency, sustained by a great
faith.

I read for a year a socialist paper in which I never
saw a single advertisement. Debts were incurred to
start it. Deficits followed like a shadow. Asked how
they went on with such a load: "Why, we have to
give a lot of time free, and beg the rest from comrades. Two in the office work three or four hours a
day after their own work is done and never take a
cent. One woman has a little money and gives all
her time. We have our pious formulas. 'He who
quickly gives, gives twice': 'Who gives himself gives
better than his coin.'" But no part of our citizenship
puts these pieties to more instant or wider use than
socialists.

If richer folk were taxed according to their means,
one half of that which thousands of socialists in our
midst are freely taxing themselves, it would be thought
an outrage and a tyranny. The sacrifices to carry on
the socialist sheet just mentioned are but a leaf from
a thick book. What goes on in that dingy office is
only a very tiny sample. In many hundreds of other
offices the same story could be told. And yet the sum
total of this press activity is itself also but a fraction

of the unpaid or poorly paid service which this cause
now inspires in the world.

One would think that devotions like these might
give some seriousness even to the jauntiest critic. It
is not for nothing that great multitudes in twenty
different countries work like that. They do not upon
principle hold out year after year in spite of perpetual
defeats and at such direct and heavy costs except
for something believed to be of life and death importance. Many of them pay this price for what they
know never can be theirs. On a bench by the Capitol
in Richmond, Virginia, I sat one night after a socialist
meeting with an old man who had seen about all one
could see of service in the Confederate cause. He had
for years given himself to build up a socialist sentiment
in that community. "I shall not live," he said, "to see
even the beginning of it. But it is a great cause." He
was one of an army, far greater than the South sent
to the field, who know that no extra penny can come
to them, but they bring their offerings just the same.

This inner spirit and soul of a great movement is
what my business friend did not see. Not seeing it,
there was only an occasion for mockery.

It was only an absurdity to this critic that men
and women who could give so much money for their
cause should claim to have a serious grievance. "What
do they want?" he asked. "Their reckless giving is
proof enough that they are getting on; otherwise they
couldn't give it." He was irritated by the aggressions
of discontent which seemed to him stupidly unjusti-
fied. "The more they get on," he argued, "the worse
they behave."

This is the fact about labor's discontent. It feeds on its own betterment. It increases because our prosperities and the general social atmosphere have created and stimulated in every class new wants and new determinations. Of a struggle that has become sacred to us Edmund Burke spoke in the English Parliament. He heard the tory taunt that the Americans were not oppressed, to which he answered: "Mr. Speaker, the question is not whether the Americans are oppressed or not; but whether they think they are."

That increasing millions in the wage receiving class have come to think as they do about economic imperfections over which men have control, constitutes our industrial problem as its political counterpart was the problem of our rebellious forebears.

These breeding dissatisfactions constitute a pressure from below that will be neither shamed nor checked by optimistic platitudes about the rise of wages. On the long curves, generation by generation, the purchasing power of labor's income has risen and the working hours are fewer. The wiser socialists know this and proclaim it.

"What, then, is the fuss about?" The fuss has to do with a thing that is wholly relative. This may have the simplest graphic expression

Let the upper line stand for the increasing income of the more prosperous and the lower line for the increasing prosperity of labor. Both have risen, but the well-to-do have gained relatively far more than the wage earner. In the United States, the distance between the large incomes and the small ones seems to have grown steadily through the century. The wage earner's contention that he should have a relatively larger share in wealth-production is justified. As he has had to fight for this in the past, he will fight for it in the future. Socialism puts a new weapon into his hands. To the old weapon of the trade union, it now adds an instrument that cuts deeper and has a longer thrust. That the masses are to use this weapon with all the force and cunning at their command is now a certainty that we need not question. Largely on account of the extent and rawness of our immigration, nowhere will they use it more ruthlessly than in the United States. No nation offers such an arena. The material advantages we put at the disposal of labor; all the stalking laxities that pass for liberty,[1] every easy facility for the widest scattering of revolutionary literature, are illustrations of the field and the occasion we open to this socialistic insurgency as it overflows into new and threatening shapes.

(II)

Especially among our more prosperous folk, if a "quiz" could be held on the causes and nature of the

---

[1] I have seen strikes in which extreme violence lasted for weeks with much shooting, and yet guns and pistols were allowed the freest selling and the saloons faithfully kept open, though they were the direct occasion of brawls, resulting in some of the most brutal cases with which the local court was plagued.

present strain and turbulence between capital and labor, I should submit as the first question this: Why does the word "scab" carry with it an indignity so poignant? To *justify* the scab or to condemn him has no part in the question. It is only sought to explain him and the savage animosities he excites. An engineer upon one of our great structures had a strike. He crushed it with strike-breakers within a week. When the work was done, I asked him about the men who took the places of those who left. "A few of them," he said, "were good fellows, but the bulk of them were skunks." I tried to learn why this impression had been made upon him, but could not get beyond this fact of explosive contempt.

In a sharp labor disturbance, I have seen a man wholly unruffled under such words as liar, coward and thief, but the monosyllable "scab" had an instantaneous effect like a dash of vitriol in the face. During the recent strike at Lawrence a generous and active friend of the strikers asked a trade union official if her organization was not really scabbing against the large body of men and women who had left the mills. I saw the woman to whom the question was put flush hot as if insulted. A little later, the tears in her eyes, she left her office saying, "I cannot stand it, I cannot stand it."

These instances are neither exceptional nor do they exaggerate by a tittle the mordant power of this word. Really to answer this question; really to see what the maddened protest implies of guilt and treachery to one's own, is a good first step in understanding what is before us of impending tasks.

A good second to the question about the scab, concerns the strike itself.   It is so incessant; reaches, year after year, in a dozen countries so many millions of people and shows no sign of abating.

What explanation have we of this?   In the twitter of the drawing-room it is "perversity," "ignorance," "wickedness," "ingratitude," and with the angered business man, it is oftenest "labor poisoned and misguided by the agitator."

That, at this date, puerilities like these should have influence with rational folk is as strange as it is ominous.   Here, as in moving pictures before us, are events involving on any calendar day far more bitterness than the sharp agonies on the down-going Titanic. In that year in the world's workhouse more than four hundred thousand men were out on long strikes and more than a million and a half in lesser ones. With their families this stands for a population like that of a larger state.   Nor is there any outer fate of compulsion like that of the Titanic disaster.

The determining majority of these strikers, according to their own law, deliberately took up the burden, the weight of which they know far better than any or all others.   The unvoiced misery of a long strike is always in the background.   It is among the wives, the weaker workers, the more timid, those that have saved no money, those that have passed their prime, and those in debt or with mortgaged homes.   It is among such as these that the main tragedy goes on, and for the thousandth time, it is entered upon.   It is these who live in the tradition of defeat and suffering caused by strikes.   Veterans are always there to

tell them that it costs. But in the face of it all, in
dreary succession, it still goes on. Of a strike at this
moment wearing itself out among English dockers,
a London reporter thus speaks:

> The suffering of the strikers' families has become so dreadful
> that the public is fairly paralyzed with horror. The streets in
> the dockyards districts are filled with hollow-eyed women and
> children, reduced almost to skeletons and so weak that they are
> hardly able to stand.
> Many have died almost wholly of starvation. The number
> of the victims is so great that the authorities and private chari-
> table organizations are unable to cope with the situation.

The official explanation that the rivalries of a few
leaders give us all the answer we need is pitiable. Of
the strike movement as a whole, it does not contain
even a paltry half-truth. I have a fairly close personal
record of eighteen strikes. Of two of them, conceiv-
ably three, the cause may be attributed to conscience-
less or imperilled leadership. But in the majority of
strikes the world over the leaders are forced to the fighting line by the workers behind them. For the most part
this leadership is a symptom and result, not a cause.

On the surface of a serious strike are conspicuous
and frisky gaieties. Youth and the irresponsible are
so much in evidence that the public does not see the
background with its silences and distress. To stagger
on, decade after decade, under a self-imposed immola-
tion like this, must have a cause not accounted for by
petulant phrases. The unexplained obstinacy with
which this costly warfare goes on is the more strange
because for half a century in several countries elaborate mechanisms have been devised to check and

soften these revolts. Arbitration, conciliation, sliding scales, trade agreements,—each in its time has been hailed as peace bringer. Each has done its little work, but, tearing through them all, the gathering unrest makes its way as if these buffers had no existence. Human tenacities like these have no explaining, except in terms of structural changes in society. A letter describing mere glimpses of this suffering in the recent English coal strike adds, "There are such depths of it, that three days were all that I could physically stand merely to observe it, and yet among those suffering most the determination to face it out was almost fierce."

This is a part of the "quiz." Why? Behind all perversities, blunders, betrayals and defeats,—why do these multitudes continue to load themselves with sacrifices so heavy? No copy-book answer can be given to these questions, but a larger answer is possible in terms of changing social and economic experience.

In the second quarter of the last century an Austrian Minister thought it an adequate account of the democratic uprising in Italy, that it was "a mere disease of envy and irreligion." He was sure that a little wholesome severity would at once restore these disturbers to the ways of obedience and common sense. This explanation and the remedy proposed now satisfy only our humor. But it is a bit of history that may well serve us as a mirror. In that feudal explanation and remedy, we may see ourselves in presence of our own industrial rebels. We now know that those early nineteenth century strikers, sick with "envy and irreligion," were fighting for political freedom. At appalling costs they were striking *politically*. Today the strike is consciously upon the field of industry. It is still the old rebelling against autocratic usages that have come first under criticism and suspicion, then under direct attack. The political uprisings that crowd the first half of the nineteenth century were full of havoc, waste and lawlessness, precisely like our own strikes. There was much vanity and self-seeking in many of the leaders then as now. But upon the whole, the political strikers of those days had the valor and disinterestedness which those must have, who break the hardened conventions of their time and open the ways of growth to larger and freer life.

In those earlier days, the enemy at which the political strikers aimed was arbitrary authority. It was an authority always justifying itself by whatever traditional sanctity had power over the imagination of the time;—religion, patriotism, and existing "law and order," *as interpreted by those in office*. Within these symbols, property interests and social proprieties solemnly cloaked themselves as they do today. They were not necessarily hypocrites. There is a terrible French utterance which most of us should learn by heart, "Why be a hypocrite, when it is so easy to deceive yourself?"

Whatever is precious in our private belongings leads readily to much deceiving and neither the defenders of the existing system nor those who rise against it will escape the danger in these hypocrisies. Few social groups have more frailties than political or industrial strikers. They are forever the easy butt of ridicule in their time. A classmate of Wendell Phillips told me that he saw the coming agitator practising his oratories before a glass and always had thereafter proper contempt for him. He would neither hear him speak nor consider his opinions. The test is rather contemptible, but it is probably as old as the history of man's likes and dislikes.

These periods of revolutionary change are not to be measured by frailties in their leaders. The only measure is the necessity of the movement itself. Political and religious authority had reached an intolerable stage early in the nineteenth century and enough brave men had found it out to make a life-and-death issue. For two generations, in spite of much squalid vanity and dreary demagogic play, it was a rousing struggle for an enlarged and richer human life. These wider opportunities for the mass of men were plainly impossible until the pretentious pieties of authority, arbitrarily enforced, were beaten. But arbitrary power did not then quit the scene. It slowly changed its form, and on the field of industry and commerce it grew great and held its own. Its cumulating power has now reached a climax. It stalks among us so flauntingly that millions of common folk can see it. It has passed from the speculations of students to the growling remonstrance of masses of men. In an age grown acute with democratic feeling, in days when political power or what is believed to be such is passing to the people through direct primaries, recalls and such like devices, our economic destinies seem still to be at the beck and call of elusive and shadowy authorities as ruthless as their predecessors. Finance and markets are their throne. They, too, have their solemn draperies, their secrecies, and neighborly interchange of inside information. Here in our midst is the real heart of monopoly power. Here are the obvious sources of that ludicrous overloading of individuals with wealth. The Power of Kings has not been greater, but it is the unknown use of this vast power, its essentially arbitrary character, that the people again have come to challenge. It seems to them in very deadly conflict with every essential of real liberty. Multitudes, no longer to be silenced, are everywhere asking what respect or patience they should have with a system producing day by day the *kind* of inequality now visible in the United States. Especially are they asking about the measure and uses of this power which one or two per cent of the people now coin for themselves. They no longer ask, but know that democracy, or any real approach to it, is impossible until these privileged economic resources are themselves in some sense democratized. Multitudes now believe that the wage system is but an instrument in the hands of these powers. Of the dizzy heights of finance and credit labor knows nothing, and even special students war with each other over its most elemental explanation; but of the "wage system" the worker has his own opinion, founded on experience. Labor therefore begins its rebellion at this point. It is striking at the kind of power that appears through this wage system. Its very ignorance of the power behind, deepens its suspicions. But for us just now, it is a dangerous obliquity not to recognize that capitalists cannot continue to work those forces in the old arbitrary spirit. If they insist upon this at the points (as in public utilities) directly and sensitively touching the general welfare, such managers will create their own trouble, and every day they will more and more create it. They will themselves be responsible for it, because they insist upon a method and, above all, upon a spirit that is outgrown. *At these more developed stages* in the wage system, there is from now on not a step toward security or progress, unless labor (as well as the public) is allowed some voice in management. This is the lesson which every industrial autocrat has to learn. Strictly on this issue, the side of the striker is as sacred as any struggling reform in human history. It has long been as sacred as at present, but the practically eventful fact now is that millions of wage earners have become sensitively conscious of the situation. They need no more evidence that the old wage method arbitrarily enforced shuts them too sharply out of privileges and rights that should be theirs. They are so convinced of this, and the army of them has grown so great, as to constitute a problem that no advanced society will safely ignore.

Hundreds of employers in the world, and a few great ones, are admitting all this and doing their best to act upon it. They are creating organs through which labor may have its representation in management. This frankly *assumes* that in highly organized industries, arbitrary wage systems have had their day. It is popularly seen that our age is supremely the age of industrial organization. If it is that, why should labor be excluded from its benefits? But of more significance still is it that the new principle of progressively democratized management demands the education of employer and laborer alike. Now the education of labor cannot longer be kept outside this common organization. It may go on in excluded and hostile areas with all the dangers that imports. Or it may go on in essential and increasing partnership with management.

To set our faces henceforth in this direction, to understand that this inclusive association, though it take a century, is the way of safety and the way of growth, is the lesson to be learned, especially in the United States. One of the most successful of English business men now in Parliament recently spent six weeks in this country. He saw a great many of our larger employers. I heard him asked about his impressions. One of them was this. "So many of your big men don't seem to me to realize in the least what is happening."

Let us begin by avoiding the blunder of that autocrat in Austria, that our present insurrection is "a mere disease of envy and irreligion." This is not in the least "what is happening." The harsh and mutinous protest of our I. W. W. is to be judged solely in its relation to a vastly larger democratic rising against the absolutism and masked economic privilege of our own day. Cynical men of the world will make light of this belief of the many. It will be so easy for them to show the muddled misconceptions in the "mass-conviction," but for what we have here in hand, it is enough that the conviction is real and that it has won alliances and quite strength enough to make its reactions felt in our political life.

V

A HISTORY OF DISAPPOINTMENT

IF the entire movement known as Socialism (including its newer and more audacious forms) is to be studied with any profit, it must be measured by other competing attempts to remedy evils and inequalities against which modern society has risen. Neither Socialism nor Syndicalism is alone in the field against the recognized facts of social injustice. In forms public and private, compulsory and voluntary, we have at last an accessible record of classified attempts to check and to remove these ills. Socialism owes much of its vigor and achievement to the conviction that these previous attempts have failed because too exclusively in control of "the master class," and its interests. It is not open to question that the history of reform is the history of disappointment. It is as if nature could not get its newer and harder tasks performed without overloading man with expectation and hope. From the upper flights of these expectations, probably no instance can be given of reform in religion, politics, or education whose ripening fruit matched in the slightest the vehement confidence from which the reform sprang. This is not only true of the very greatest of the world's inspirers: it is not only true of men of emotional impelling like St. Simon, Fourier, or Mazzini: it is true of those as cool and disciplined as John Stuart Mill and Richard Cobden.

Compared with Mills' splendid hopes for representative government (and what it "would hasten of great and fundamental reforms"), the actual thing obtained looks pallid enough.

Here in the United States every step in the swift coming of direct primaries, initiative, referendum, and recall records the disappointment of our people with legislative and legal procedure. It is a fact that effective political power has been kept from the people. It is the gist of this new protest that the broad, inclusive interests have been in no vital sense "represented." To get this representation is now a world fight. Everywhere it is seen that if democracy is to be real it must have a far broader *economic* basis. This is not a cry of the cranks alone. It appears among the very ablest students of politics. In the stiff volumes of Ostrogorski,[1] which won high praise from James Bryce, our own sinning against genuine representation is set down in pages cruel with veracity. In his recent study, *Democracy and the Party System*, a single passage from his concluding chapter shows us how he would broaden these economic foundations of our political life. He sees how the people's choice is choked and defeated in the Senate—Federal and State. He asserts that the weaker economic interests have no representation there. He then adds:

Conflicts are getting more and more bitter, clouds are gathering thick in the social sky, and it is on the arbitraments of the Senate that social peace will depend. But how can fair judgment be secured if the representation of economic interests in

[1] *Democracy and the organization of Political Parties*, Macmillan.

the Senate is not made broader? And how can such a representation be established?

I think it could be done, and without breaking the old framework of the Senate. Its basis should remain unchanged, every State, large and small, keeping its two representatives in the high Federal chamber. But to these Senators should be added Associate Senators representing directly and specially the great social and economic forces of the country—chambers of commerce, boards of trade, manufacturers' associations, trades unions, granges, churches,—not as ecclesiastical but as great social organizations,—universities, bar associations, etc. Every great national interest would have its legitimate spokesman in the high assembly, and their knowledge of the special conditions with which they are connected would bring these latter to light before the Senate and the country. The coördination of struggling economic forces, so far as it depends on legislation, would be promoted in a spirit of fairness. The trusts themselves could plead their cause, they would only be challenged to come out in the open instead of working out their ends underhand as now. Organized labor too should have the opportunity and obligation of stating and of proving its case.

The spirit of this passage does not differ from scores of passages in syndicalist writing—as, for example, this, which just appears in the English organ:

Parliament is merely the organ of the existing Capitalist Class, and with the inevitable decay and passing away of that class as a class, Parliament itself must also wither and decay with it. . . . This, in fact, is already the condition of Parliament. It is an organism which, having fulfilled its mission in life, is now naturally withering and passing away before our eyes.

The reactions in this disappointment are far deeper than that against representative government. The feeling has deepened that, until the economic grip of

capital is loosened, reforms in every variety will fail
to reach the heart of the disorder.

Again, two generations have passed since Cobden's
glowing prophecies about freedom applied to trade. If
he could repeat his long journey today, it would be to
look upon a greedy scramble for market restrictions
scarcely without exception. We know what Thomas
Jefferson thought that popular educative agencies,
such as public libraries, would bring about. We have
these institutions far beyond his dream. In Massachusetts scarcely a hamlet is so small as to be without its
public library. Some commonplace towns have two or
three, and one town upon Cape Cod has five. These
and the people's schools have wrought their service,
but every deeper human and social problem remains
about as obstinate as before. So little has universal
suffrage met the earlier hopes, that half the educated
people one meets distrust it, and would hail its restric-
tion with downright satisfaction. We turn back to the
first writers upon some new phase of education,—let
us say, manual training or the kindergarten. The
first messages were like a new and conquering religion.
They had the promise of some stately reconstruction
which a single generation might bring about. In
Cambridge, I have just listened to two very high
authorities on these special forms of training. They
know the changes these have brought about, and they
do not undervalue them, but their estimates are very
cool and balanced. Another lecturer was on fire with
the new anarchistic emphasis in child rearing of
Madam Montessori. The listener guessed that after
a decade or two, he also would speak calmly and

more critically about this latest educational innovation.

And thus it is with the whole galaxy of reforms. I listened to the first heralds in Massachusetts of the Australian Ballot. They seemed at the time to offer a fundamental cure for our political ills. The reform has corrected some evils. It has brought some bettering. More than this cannot be said.

If we pass directly to the "Social Question," the story does not change. For more than a century, we have had in the United States above two hundred costly colonizing experiments in which some thousands of men and women staked their all to prove the new and better ways in genuine brotherhood. Unless held by religious faiths, these brave ventures have had an average life of less than three years. With perhaps two exceptions, that prove little, even the religious ones have almost vanished.

Long since the socialists learned to deride and disclaim them, but not until two generations had made it obvious that success did not lie that way. When experience had well proved their failure, we were told: "Of course scattered colonies in a continent of capitalism can not endure. We must work through the social whole. We must first capture and reform the continent." This history of frustrated hopes has the more significance because these "Apart Colonies" have had every variety of form in the whole gamut of social scheming; Anarchist, Socialist, Communist and now Single Tax. Their constitutions, programs, and practical policies show much diversity, and yet the shades of defeat are over them all, as colonies.

Not one of these could hold its own against the hated competitive system. Not one of them could retain the most enterprising and virile of its youth. Not one of them could match in the slightest the stimulating opportunities for larger and a richer life which a capitalistic society, in spite of its sins, still offers.

In another series of reforms, the disappointment has been less final, but very real. For half a century heroic groups have gathered about "arbitration," "conciliation," "profit sharing," "sliding scales," and "bonus systems," and these have paid their way, some of them richly. Each has left its increment of good which a wiser future will put to use and learn to integrate with other agencies. But these tiny deposits to our assets bear but a ghostly likeness to those first high-hearted hopes.[1] The older literature of arbitration and profit-sharing is fired with confident anticipation that a "solution" has been found; an open way along which capital and labor, arm in arm, may pass to early and permanent peace. After a generation of "voluntary arbitration" had shown with chilling proof that some of the deepest difficulties in the wage relation were beyond the reach of this contrivance, then New Zealand appeared with her famous bill adding "compulsion." By good luck, it came in days of rising prosperity when labor had its fairest chances. It was then that one of the most fearless and gallant of our citizens, Henry D. Lloyd, brought back his story of "A Country Without Strikes." It was an

[1] In a Bulletin of the Department of Labor for January, 1912, is an admirable summary of the results of arbitration.

epic of hope, reflecting upon every page his own generous spirit. But labor there today shows a surly disposition. In some of the severer conflicts, the act is so feared that settlement is sought outside the act. Yet Mr. Reeves, its author, told a Boston audience that the act was conceived to meet this very class of strikes.[1]

After watching the workings of the act for several years, trade unions in England and the United States bluntly and stubbornly refuse their approval, while Socialists of prominence like Charles Edward Russell have only boisterous ridicule for the act.

Let it be said again that these reforms have "paid their way." Utter failure is not to be charged against them. As in Emerson's poem, these reforms, like the Dervish, have not brought diadems; their offering was only homely and useful fruits. It is our habit to exclaim, "But if men do not expect diadems, they will not give themselves greatly and pluckily to their tasks." For herbs and apples, they will not suffer as Mazzini suffered. Hauntingly before him he must see the shining towers beneath which dwells his "cleansed and perfected Republic." One wonders if he would have starved and risked his life an hundred times for the actual Italy of 1912, with its war against Tripoli. Would those who bore all the weary buffeting in early trade union organization have done it for the existing American Federation of Labor? One chief source of I. W. W. rebelling is the embittered sense

[1] Recently a New Zealander, W. D. Stewart, and an American economist, Professor Le Rossignol, have given us the sobered estimate of this act in their volume, *State Socialism in New Zealand*.

of miscarriage and shattered hopes in that large majority to which the trade union has brought so little.

In the same spirit of distrust, the trade union itself rebels against the proffered benefactions of capital.

The recent action of some forty thousand brewery workers has an unmistakable meaning. There was no stampeding of minorities; no thought of violence, or even haste. With cool deliberation and by overwhelming majorities, this powerful labor body refused to accept one of the most liberal Compensation Funds ever offered to labor. After its provisions had been published in their own official organ,[1] a month was given to discussion with communications pro and con, like the long discussion of sabotage and the referendum vote in the New York Call. Another month was given to the vote. Nearly twenty-three thousand men voted against the Compensation and Old Age Pension offer, although each beneficiary was still free to choose the common law or statutory remedy. Every old offense of "contributory negligence," "fellow servant defense," and "assumption of risk," had been discarded. The benefits were to begin *ten years* earlier than under the German State Insurance,—a concession of the utmost importance.

These labor men had learned, too, that not one injury in five secured compensation under present conditions. They knew well the long and uncertain delays, even when they won the case, as they knew the bleeding fees of the private lawyers. Not a feature of all this but had been amply discussed. There

[1] See *Brauerei-Arbeiter Zeitung*, Feb. 3, 1912.

was no shadow of doubt that the employers would promptly pay the benefits.

Of what were the benefits to consist?

Every brewery-worker injured in connection with his work would receive a specified, liberal, compensation of sixty-five per cent of the wages he would otherwise have earned during the period of his disability, or that in the event of his killing in connection with his work his dependents, if any, would receive, in lump sum or in *pro rata* payments as the Board of Directors and Award might deem best in each case, the equivalent of sixty-five per cent of the victim's wages for three hundred weeks, or practically six years—to the amount of not more than $3,400.[1]

One hundred and eighty-one unions voted against the plan. There is nothing inscrutable about this, even to the employers who say: "They think we are Greeks bearing gifts." That is the explanation. This strong and well-paid labor organization has become so far socialist, so far "class conscious," that it dreads every measure which identifies its interests those of the master class. This labor organization knows that it is very far in the future before the Government in this country will give them anything comparable to what the employers offered. Yet they refuse, preferring freedom to fight for their cause unimpeded, when and how they choose. This is the syndicalist spirit, and with the growth of Socialism, it becomes daily more and more the spirit of the trade union. It is this spirit that refuses the New Zealand Arbitration Act, and the "incorporation" of their

[1] The details of this may all be found in *The American Underwriter*, April, 1912. There was obviously the fear of a " joker " which in some way was believed to cripple their freedom of action.

unions. It is this spirit that turns them like one man against "court injunctions" and deepens their suspicion against the courts themselves.

In trying to account for a world impulse like Socialism and even more for one like Syndicalism with its theoretic fascinations and the bravado of its practice, we may save ourselves much trouble if these balked hopes in the history of reform are kept in mind. In the half dozen countries where Syndicalism has made itself really felt—where, as "proletariat" or the "fourth estate," it has made men stop to listen and reflect, we shall find the same story of disappointed expectations. Politicians of every ilk and shade had promised results that did not come. Incoming governments held out hopes that were not realized. Wherever these disappointments reach a certain portion of the wage earners, Syndicalism gets its first expression. It began in France, where labor unions were so organized as to secure political influence, the results of which could be tested:—where very few years were enough to show what politics could do for them and what it could not do. It began when the older unions (craft organizations) had come to see how little they had done or were likely to do for their own uplifting. Many a union had won advantages for itself, but these were always checked by the employer's use of new machinery *plus* easy access to tenfold larger numbers outside the unions, always there, to keep wages low. The part played by several of these French unions led, moreover, to a momentous discovery that economic forces, transportation and electricity were so safely in the hands of the workers that they might use them to gain their objects far more directly than through the tedious ways of politics.[1]

The very right to organize had been withheld as late as 1884. When permission came, unions burst into such efflorescence that in ten years, more than two thousand active organizations were a part of the industrial and political life of the nation. The very attempt to crib them had turned them over to socialist influence. This meant political action. They captured towns by the score. Besides mayors and local officials, they sent their own men to the Chamber of Deputies and were the first in Europe to count Socialists among the Ministers of State.

Ten years ago, I visited several of these communes under socialist administration, hearing from Socialists for the first time the pique and irritation because their officials were doing so little for the cause. I have seen no socialist city with even six months' experience in the United States, where this same precocious complaint could not be heard. It is shallow and unfair criticism, but it shows us the sources of Syndicalism.

Two or three years later it was written: "We Socialists in ninety Communes have benches full of Deputies and two Members of the Government, but what have they done for Socialism? They are busy, most of them, explaining why they can do nothing. One critic said, 'The only talent they had developed was *"le talent de s'execuser"*; it is all talk, talk.'" Thus out of the sorrow or the rage of disappointment

[1] The word syndicalism is the counterpart of our own term trade unionism.

Syndicalism was born. It was only a more concrete and acute form of that chagrin at the failure of parliaments and legislatures which the people of many countries have come to feel, and none more rebelliously than we in the United States.

It is thus not alone the revelation that politics and trade unions work so feebly and so tardily, Socialism also brought its own discouragements, to those who are now Syndicalists. Socialism is long enough in the field to have furnished its own "history of disappointment."

Socialism has democratized hope, and it is nobly to its credit that it has done this; but it will also be one of its most enduring and exacting disciplines. If it incites lively anticipations, they must be satisfied. The socialist impeachment has smeared the existing order as with pitch, and at the same time fixed all eyes on its own radiant picture of the world that is to be when "land and the tools are restored to those who labor."

In nothing is Socialism more useful than that it has carried new ardors of expectation and faith to the huddled masses lower in the scale. It has done this at the very time when these masses refuse longer to be put off with other worldly substitutes. That we have come so near accepting poverty, unemployment, prostitution and sweated wages as practical fatalities which must always abide with us, has as little moral excuse as to take small pox or dirty milk as fatalities. Socialism, as much as any other single influence, has forced on the coming war against these immemorial dishonors. These with economic changes have made this socialist criticism and arousing possible. The city and industrial center have gathered the workers where they can be reached by the new method. These centers have made organization possible. A thousand socialist papers and an enormous pamphlet literature are in active circulation.

Whatever else may be said of this literature, it stimulates belief in possible social changes that shall enlarge opportunity and distribute economic values with more equal hand. But Socialism will have to pay the same penalty that those have always paid who promise too much. The deepest causes of Syndicalism are economic, but its more obvious and proximate origin lies in these frustrated hopes. It is the child of disillusionment. Those who began it had been over-promised or had come to expect of politics, of the trade union, and of the Socialism then in vogue, far more than each or all of them could deliver.

Out of the chagrin, hopes that no defeat can extinguish in the heart of youth took another flight. The goal toward which it turns is much the same, but the route and the means through which the journey must be made differ from those of politics, of trade unions and of Socialism, as these have hitherto been known. Yet in studying Syndicalism, we are still dealing with labor organization, though it has changed its emphasis and form. We are still occupied with politics, though its whole basis of representation is transformed. Neither are we quite cut loose from Socialism.

What most concerns us in this study and what is at the same time most beset with perplexity is sufficiently to differentiate Syndicalism and preserve the roots that still inhere in the mother trunk from which it springs.

No intelligent step in this study seems to me possible unless the larger movement is first considered. A powerful contingent of our trade unions is now desperately defending itself before the public. Never were so many well-to-do folk more relentless in their animosity toward trade unions than at the present moment. Never was labor [1] so outspoken in its bitterness against the imperfections of the wage system. There is nowhere a sign that this hostility is lessening. The organized and articulate part of labor never showed more moody distrust of all those agencies meant for peace between capital and labor.

More and more our most momentous strikes are at bottom for "recognition." The points of conflict are thrown out nearer the capitalistic citadel of *management*. The present working of the wage system is challenged. Certain portions of this system as arbitrarily managed are obviously breaking up before our eyes.

Syndicalism is the outer, more daring and reckless labor section in this attack.

[1] To save tedious qualifications the word "labor" will be freely used in this volume for the "wage earner."

VI

FORERUNNERS OF THE I. W. W.

No one has given us a deeper or truer perspective through which we may see labor's long struggle to organize than Beatrice and Sidney Webb. With exhaustive thoroughness, they show in the third chapter of their *History of Trade Unionism* a brief, throbbing period like that of our Knights of Labor. It is a passionate moment that fuses labor, so precisely in the spirit of our I. W. W., that we seem to be reading sentence by sentence the latest syndicalist utterance. There was breathless expectation that capitalism was doomed. It is an even eighty years since Owen and his followers proposed—almost to the last detail— all that our I. W. W. now urge,—"eliminate politics, band labor together at the bottom with light dues or no dues at all, with power decentralized, the general strike, and the dream of the coöperative commonwealth." The "means of production" were, of course, to be "taken over" but "were to become the property not of the whole community, but of the particular set of workers who used them. The trade unions were to be transformed into 'national companies' to carry on all the manufactures. The agricultural union was to take possession of the land, the miners' union of the mines, the textile unions of the factories. Each trade was to be carried on by its particular trade union, centralized into one 'grand lodge.'"

Syndicalism at its best has got far beyond this naïve proposal that miners are alone to own and dispose of the product; that railway employees, textile workers and shoemakers are each to have exclusive possession of the industry in which they happen just then to be working. Little reflection is needed to show that this would leave us with the same old difficulties of privileged and parasitic groups. While one finds plenty of youthful Syndicalists who have not got beyond this artless conception, the more mature thought is of a "federated administration" that shall distribute unearned increment and advantage to the social whole. Here in some form is the "Grand Lodge" of Owen's days.

In contagious enthusiasm and rapidity of growth, this forerunner far outmatches anything yet accomplished by modern Syndicalism. More than four hundred thousand workers were grouped into fellowship fired with expectation of some great oncoming event. So quick was the exhaustion, that the story is one of the most pathetic in labor annals.

Of the real power of capitalistic industry, there seems to have been, even among the leaders, no slightest intimation, and quite as little sense of the law and its influence over property rights. This over-heated movement left its own priceless legacy of coöperative impulse, though with only faintest resemblance to the expected reformation.

Adequately to fill out these origins, Chartism also would claim notice. This is usually described as a political uprising and, therefore anti-Syndicalist. But it had also its outcry against politics. There was direct onslaught against actual politicians; the same emphasis on the economic aspects—the same appeal to the entire labor mass. Disraeli's *Sybil*, written in this period, has a passage,[1] to which I have seen several references in syndicalist sheets. It has the ring of the I. W. W. orator in every line. "Hope had deserted the laboring classes: they had no confidence in any future of the existing system. Their organization, *independent of the political system* of the Chartists, was complete. Every trade had its union, and every union its lodge in every town and its central committee in every district.

"Every engine was stopped, the plug was driven out of every boiler, every fire was extinguished, every man was turned out. The decree went forth that labor was to cease until the charter was the law of the land; the mine and the mill, the foundry and the loomshop, were, until that consummation, to be idle; nor was the mighty pause to be confined to these great enterprises. Every trade of every kind and description was to be stopped—tailor and cobbler, brushmaker and sweep, tinker and carter, mason and builder, all, all."

The next link is the "International" of the early sixties. The "General Rules" of this body throw the entire responsibility for their emancipation upon the "working classes." It is to be an *economic* emancipation. "Solidarity of labor" is the shibboleth.

The founder of French Syndicalism expressly acknowledges the parenthood of the International,[2] as

---

[1] Quoted in Harley's *Syndicalism*. The words which I put in italics show the familiar economic reaction against sectional attempts to make too much of political hopes.

[2] Pelloutier at the Fourth Congress of the Bourses du Travail.

also does Emil Pouget.[1] But for more direct light
upon the I. W. W. our own recent labor history is
still more useful.

In the midst of a strike, I heard a studious and
conscientious journalist ask a leader busy with the
strike, how one could best "book up" on the history
of the I. W. W. The reply came, "Study the Knights
of Labor first; most of it is there." He qualified this
later, but there is quite truth enough in the hurried
suggestion to merit attention. From the early thir-
ties, labor unions had felt the weakness of isolation
and there was consequent striving for such federation
as would band these scattered bodies into state and
national organizations. This especially appears after
periods of defeat. In no industry has defeat been
brought home to the workers with more tragic fre-
quency than in the clothing trade. From these discouragements and from the brain of one of the most
thoughtful men the labor movement has produced in
the United States, M. S. Stephens, the "Knights of
Labor" sprang. His own union among the garment
workers had had a bitter history, ending at last in
failure. Like Henry George, Stephens had traveled
widely, spending several years on the Pacific Coast.
With rare gifts for reflective observation, he turned
every experience to good account. He was one of the
first to see the hopelessness of labor's struggle, if
dependence were placed alone on the separate craft
union. His observations on this point sound like an
I. W. W. orator attacking the groundwork of existing
unions. He dreamed of a federation which should

[1] *Le parti du travail.*

sweep in the millions, giving labor the "full united strength of associated manhood." In his house in Philadelphia, late in 1869, this large desire was embodied in the plan, solemnly named "The Noble and Holy Order of the Knights of Labor." "Noble" and "Holy" were soon dropped, and the Knights of Labor entered upon their work as a secret order with much ceremonial pomp, which brought its own penalties in the end. As clearly as Fourier and Marx saw the coming of the great organization in business, Stephens noted the rapid rise of these new powers that followed so swiftly after the Civil War. If capital was to have these enormous advantages, labor must secure them or be crushed. This was his problem. Every member received for instruction the following appeal:

Labor is noble and holy. To defend it from degradation; to divest it of the evils to body, mind, and estate which ignorance and greed have imposed; to rescue the toiler from the grasp of the selfish,—is a work worthy of the noblest and best of our race. . . . We mean no conflict with legitimate enterprise, no antagonism to necessary capital; but men, in their haste and greed, blinded by self-interests, overlook the interests of others, and sometimes violate the rights of those they deem helpless. We mean to uphold the dignity of labor, to affirm the nobility of all who earn their bread by the sweat of their brows. We mean to create a healthy public opinion on the subject of labor (the only creator of values), and the justice of its receiving a full, just share of the values or capital it has created.

This has not the definiteness of Syndicalism as now stated. In the words, "We mean no conflict with legitimate enterprise, no antagonism to necessary capital"—we have a phrasing which every I. W. W.

follower would challenge. To him there is no "necessary capital" except that which society itself owns.

But like the I. W. W., Stephens looked toward the complete extirpation of the wage system. To this end, decades of educational effort were to be made through the organs created by this new order. As in the I. W. W., hostility was shown to "intellectuals." Physicians,[1] politicians, and lawyers were excluded:— the lawyers because they were so largely a parasitic class like liquor-dealers, who were also excluded.

After 1872, beginning with plumbers and painters, a steady increase of carpenters, masons, machinists, steel makers, weavers, fell into line. State after state joined with an ever larger variety of craft unions, until at Richmond in 1886, nearly nine thousand trade unions had gathered under the banners of the Knights of Labor. But with each mounting step, troubles followed. Every added thousand brought its increment of conflict. A local union, or even all the unions in a given trade, had interests in common. The "local" understood those interests and could define and act upon them far more intelligently than any distant official body.

It thrilled like a trumpet note to hear that "the heart of labor beats with a common throb," that "its interests are one with the all-embracing brotherhood of toil"; but when a plague of petty strikes broke out in 1880–1, the responsible officials were frightened. Mr. Powderly was then "General Master Workman." He sent out a pathetic protest, precisely as the French

[1] The doctors were later admitted. The "Secrecy" of the order accounted in part for these exclusions.

Syndicalist Lagardelle has recently cried out for a
"revision of the facts and the ideas" of his order.
"After a glorious beginning," he says, "we find ourselves faced with what generally results from forced
marches—complete exhaustion." English Syndicalism, since the pitiable failure of the dockers' strike,
is eating the same bitter fruit. The over-stimulated
activity of the strike will enfeeble the I. W. W. as
it did the Knights of Labor. The power of the strike
is in its restraint, not in its profusion.

But the greater lesson is that the Knights of
Labor, like the I. W. W., brought to the front
an ideal relationship of labor that does not stand
the strain put upon it. It is pleasant to say that
the interests of Western lumbermen are one with
those of New Jersey Glass Blowers, but a conflict
with employers in the lumber camp may prove within
a week that, for the fighting moment, they have
nothing in common with far-off glass blowers or with
labor in an hundred other removed industries. Soon
after 1880, this actual conflict of interests between
craft unions and the Knights of Labor set in with
increasing violence. It was found that "craft autonomy" had its own sturdy vitality. In the first
high enthusiasms, organizers were sent broadcast to
create new unions.[1] They were chartered and set on
their way irrespective of any grievance with employer, past or present. One or two years passed when
it slowly became clear to the members that their

---

[1] Mr. Walling writes in the *New Review*, Jan. 18, "Revolutionary
unionists conclude that *the cure for lost strikes is more strikes;* strikes
more frequent, more aggressive, and on a larger scale."

regular dues were paid solely to assist unknown and far-off strikers of whose case they knew nothing except through reporters whose interest it was to see that dues were collected. Rumors followed that many of these strikes were from inner jurisdictional feuds or from local rivalries between envious leaders. Was hard-earned money to be paid by labor in Cincinnati to doubtful quarrels in some New England "local"? Hundreds of unions fell away, one after another, because the resonant phrases about "labor's united interests" came to be questioned and then defied. When errors of judgment are made or violent passions lead, it is a wild folly to insist that "labor's cause is always sacred against the employer." The sole measure of labor's common interest is the soundness and justice of its cause. There are no "common interests of labor, right or wrong," any more than there is a decent patriotism, "right or wrong."

In the height of the Knights of Labor ascendency, I stopped off the train in a New England textile town to inquire about a strike then raging. It was on the slippery edges of defeat. It was from a trade unionist that I heard at once, "We have put our foot in it. We thought the employers were making a thirty per cent profit and we acted on that, and now we have got perfectly good evidence that they are not making seven per cent, and we've got to get out of the scrape as best we can." There have been quite uncounted thousands of such strikes. A few years later, conflicts in the K. of L. became so frequent that unions by scores dropped from their allegiance and the first intimations of a new order, The American Federation of Labor, were heard. This body restored again the more localized power in the trade union.

The Knights of Labor had in its Constitution for Local Assemblies lines calling for "the grand union of all who toil, regardless of sex, of creed, or of color," in the exact vein of Mr. Haywood's latest speech. This had an emotional value like that of a new religion, until the stress of an actual strike revealed the real intensities of local self-interest as against that sublime but shadowy vision,—"the brotherhood of labor as wide as the world, as linked as a chain, with no enemy but the master class."

This level, horizontal identification of labor interests as against all others, deified into a principle of action, wrecked the Knights of Labor, as it will wreck any conceivable body which attempts its application to the bread and butter tasks of daily life. The wage scale of labor in the world varies from at least six dollars a day to five cents a day. Groups of turbaned and dusky creatures from the far East who received in India less than ten cents daily, now work (timidly because always in risk of their lives) up and down the Pacific Coast. With the swift mobilities of steam navigation this contact between a ten-cent standard and a two-or-three-dollar standard has in it more fatalities of enraged enmity than any which exist between "capital and labor." I have seen negroes working in the lower South for sixty cents daily, and this during less than half the days of the year. What "solidarity" is there between these and Butte miners? What acknowledged "solidarity" was there at the Lawrence strike between the lower polyglot workers and the best paid English labor in the mills? [1] I heard no bitterer outbursts there than between members of these two groups. If this antagonism asserts itself when the difference in wages is less than fifty per cent, what must it be between those separated by three or four hundred per cent?

In 1880, the rents in the K. of L. organization were so threatening that the propensity to strike was acknowledged by the ablest leaders to be so perilous as to require immediate attention. Two years later these men ask that the Constitution be thoroughly overhauled. Schism was rife. Threats of withdrawal came in from all quarters. Though the radical element prevailed at this moment, it brought from Grand Master Powderly the following warning, which reads precisely like warnings which began to be heard in France two years ago. Powderly said:

> One cause for the tidal wave of strikes that has swept over our Order comes from the exaggerated reports of the strength of the Order, numerically and financially, given by many of our organizers. Such a course may lead men into the Order, but by a path that leads them out again; for, as soon as they become convinced that they were deceived, they lose confidence in the Order.

In 1884, the Knights of Labor had learned that the boycott, unless carefully restrained, was also full of peril. We hear, too, that "benefit funds" must be built up to strengthen the Order. Two years later,

---

[1] This requires one modification. Individual men and women in receipt of high wages quit work from sympathy in many strikes. It is one of the noblest features in scores of great contests. To suppose, however, that this can be generalized into a universal fact and made the basis of a policy of social reconstruction is an illusion.

strikes were so restricted in the proposals of the chief committee as to bring out the retort from radical members that the Order was to be deprived of its one great weapon.[1] Mr. Powderly's most desperate final effort was to persuade the membership to find other means to settle labor disputes. That the strike and boycott had invaluable uses was never questioned, but these few arduous years taught every sane head upon whom responsibilities fell, that no *organization* could either live or thrive upon measures so costly and so essentially destructive.

This lesson the I. W. W. might learn from their forerunner, as they might learn some hints about the possibilities of the "General Strike" to which they turn as the last great instrument of their freedom. The Knights of Labor were less ambitious. They created an organization which lent itself to new uses of the boycott and the "sympathetic" strike. This sweeps together widely different unions into a common revolt. There was much eloquence expended upon its possibilities. The "sympathetic strike" was but a fine practical illustration of their noble motto: "An injury to one is the injury to all." In three successive

---

[1] The words of the proposed amendment were as follows:

That no strike shall be entered upon or sanctioned by any Local, Trade, District, or State Assembly, when aid, financial or otherwise, may be required from outside such Assembly, until the General Executive Board shall have been represented by one or more of its members, or assistants, in an effort to settle the pending difficulty by arbitration, and then only by order of the General Executive Board.

Any strike entered upon without such order by the General Executive Board shall receive no assistance, financial or otherwise, from the Order outside of such Assembly; nor shall any appeal to the Order for such aid be permitted.

years, 1886-7-8, this was tried at terrible cost on two railroads and among the longshoremen. It was a most sobering experience which later put the rising "Federation" on its guard.

It is from this time on that confusion and disorder play havoc with the Knights of Labor, until it gives place to its great rival now in the field, the American Federation of Labor.[1]

Because the Knights of Labor became a wreck, it does not follow as a fatality that the I. W. W. will likewise fail. Labor has learned much since then, and what is now "the great industry" has so changed as to require corresponding changes in labor policies. "As capital becomes international, as its organization becomes more compact, we too," says a Syndicalist, "must adapt ourselves to the new economic order." As a general statement, this is harmless, but it does not help us. To "internationalize the common interests of labor over against capital," is to multiply by ten every specific obstacle which wrecked the Knights of Labor. The same conflict of interests which, to their sorrow, sprang up like dragon's teeth, will increase with every widening of racial and national areas where our American Syndicalism proposes to carry the conflict.

[1] The I. W. W. show much determination to avoid the *political* disasters which befell the Knights of Labor.

VII

THE I. W. W.

LIKE the sound of a bell in the night, the "Industrial Workers of the World" strike an alarm note that seems as new and strange to us as if some unknown enemy were at the gate. Both the purpose and the weapons used are alien and uncanny to our thought. We are just becoming half wonted to Socialism, but the defiant, riotous ways of this American Syndicalism are past understanding. For its field of action it selects most unexpected points; hotels and restaurants with petrifying hints that concern the stomach of the public; then the camp of lumberjacks, north and south; small self-confident cities on the Pacific Coast, West Virginia mines, Pittsburg industries and New England textile cities, hitherto proud of their orderly records. More disconcerting still is its attack on Socialism, as we have known it. This is beset by the new comers with as much acrimony as capitalism itself. A prolific I. W. W. literature has more acrid abuse of the many prominent socialist leaders than anything appearing in capitalistic sheets.

Tit for tat, against the I. W. W. and its prevailing tactics, socialist authorities the world over are writing by far the most scathing and contemptuous criticism. This is true even in Germany where Syndicalism has secured the least hold upon the movement. A Marxian dignitary as prominent as Karl Kautsky has just taken it in hand. The entire practice of these new agitators, he tells us, is "a mere child's disease of the labor union." The most withering censure which Socialists can bestow is to call anything "bourgeois," yet Kautsky finds this word aptly descriptive. Both the theory and practice of Syndicalism "are the expression of the bourgeois spirit which has not been able to adapt itself to modern industrial conditions." He connects the activities in France, where Syndicalism was born, with the undeveloped conditions of labor unions. He thinks Austrian socialists have already got the best of the plague and other European countries will soon be free of it.

That Europe will free herself so easily from this "child's disease" is open to question, but we in this country shall not escape its discipline. The very spirit with which we fight it will, for a long time, help it. We have already added immeasurably to its strength by the use of tactics as little defensible as the practice of the I. W. W. itself. For the gravity of the movement in this country, I shall not offer general or theoretic proofs. The theory, or "philosophy," of the movement will be given, but main stress will be placed upon the practical experience of Syndicalism as it has expressed itself in the last few years.

For some weeks in Europe, I watched one of the first general strikes consciously animated by the syndicalist spirit. It was very dumfounding at that time to hear well-known socialists and trade union veterans both classed as "parasites" and "fakers." It was a violent "sympathetic strike quite in the ordinary style but one to which the name "general"

was added. This is the great weapon of the new
propaganda. After interminable discussion it was
adopted by that powerful body in Paris, the "General
Confederation of Labor." A few years after its
formation in 1895, I again saw a sharp contest directed by that body under syndicalist leadership.
This led me to gather the literature available at that
time, of which some account will be given in other
chapters. In 1903, I was asked by the late Commissioner of Labor, Carroll D. Wright, to report to him
confidentially upon the strike in Colorado of the
Western Federation of Miners.

In the murky terrors of that miners' strike, the
vehement and practical thing called I. W. W. had its
birth. Grimy and hot, it rose there as from a sulphur-
ous pit. It is insufficient testimony, but one of the
more daring leaders in that strike assured me that
not one of them ever heard of "Syndicalism" as for
ten years it had been known in Europe. He said,
"One or two of us knew that trade unions were called
Syndicates in France, and that *sabotage* meant some
sort of a row with the boss, in which labor got back at
him with new tricks. It enabled the men to hold on
to their jobs while the strike was still carried on 'at
the point of production.'" Here they could quietly
bring worse damage to the employer. The same in-
formant has since assured me "The I. W. W. was
hammered out in the fires of that conflict." So far
as origins have value, the source of the Western Federation of Miners and its stormy history must have
brief notice. The most rugged personality it has produced is that of William D. Haywood, who was amused

that any one should think the mild disturbance at
Lawrence, Mass., really serious. It was at most
like a scrimmage among ladies. But Colorado, he
said, "was the real thing, that was a *man's fight.*"
Amidst the ranklings at Lawrence, a citizen cried out,
"What have we done that a pack of ignorant foreigners should hold us by the throat?"

The first fact in the "man's fight" from Cœur
d'Alene in 1894, to Cripple Creek in 1903-4 is that
"foreigners" neither led it nor were very conspicuous
in it. It was as "American" as the Republican Party.
This "Western Federation" began in Butte, Montana,
in the spring of 1893. In section 2 of its Constitution
are these lines:

"The objects of this organization shall be to unite
the various persons working in and around the mines,
mills, and smelters into one central body, to practice
those virtues that adorn society, and remind man of
his duty to his fellow man, the elevation of his position,
and the maintenance of the rights of the workers."

In a statement signed by the President, Charles
Moyer, and by the Secretary-Treasurer, William D.
Haywood, we read:

"Previous to an applicant being initiated to membership in the Western Federation of Miners or taking
the obligation, the following assurance is made:

"This body exacts no pledge or obligation which in
any way conflicts with the duty you owe to your God,
your country, or your fellow-man."

These verbal pieties staged for the public ear, are
not really worse than some of the appeals to the
"dignity of the law," to "true Americanism," to "the

honor of the flag," made by the employers at a time
when they were practicing the most wily form of lawlessness. They are even less repulsive than letters
from judges, governors, attorney-generals, published
in Senate Document Numbers 86, and 163, of the
Fifty-eighth Congress (second session) showing with
what plump material favors the loyalty of these
gentlemen was secured by the railroads. Some are
from the Supreme Court Chambers—as. for example,
this:

> I thank you most sincerely for your favor. I asked Mr. ——
> to speak to you, because he knew better than anyone else what
> I had done for the railroad attorneys, and stand ready to do
> whenever I can. I hope to be able to prove my appreciation of
> this favor.
>
> Yours very truly,
>
> ————

As this wretched business is long past, I withhold all
names, but they stand there in the Senate record with
others to jog the memories of those who assured us
for many years that railroad passes had no perverting
influence on the action of those who received them.

On the dingy background of a lawlessness that included employers and miners alike, these official
solemnities recall the piety of the great pirate Haw-
kins, naming his flagship *The Jesus.*[1]

These unpleasant notes are not recorded here to
excuse the succession of inhuman savageries of which
some members of the Western Federation of Miners
were plainly guilty. On both sides there were years

---

[1] See Channing's *History of the United States*, Vol. I, p. 116, for this
and other gems of the same character.

of frontier warfare with every characteristic of war except its public and official sanction. It is a story that reads like the vandalisms connected with our early "Whiskey Rebellion" as recorded in Mc-Master's second volume of his History.

The men owning large mining properties and transportation systems in those regions did not propose to have groups of socialistic trade unions endanger these values. Millions were listed on the stock market liable to tumble if investors were frightened and credit impaired. Nothing is more cruel or more lawless than great properties if thoroughly intimidated. In the midst of this struggle a lawyer, fighting for these interests, said openly, "Law or no law, we will not have a lot of thugs interfere with our business."

There is no such study of social guilt as that revealed very generally in this country during serious strikes. Police duties which belong strictly to public authorities are turned over to owners of private property. Thus instantly appear upon the scene detectives, spies, and imported strike-breakers, among whom (as in this instance) are lawless and desperate characters. Deliberately, we permit and sanction this procedure, certain to create upon the spot every condition out of which insane hatreds and violence are bred. Both origin and cause are thus to large extent social rather than individual. This burden of guilt and responsibility society must bear, with every unhappy consequence, until these private agencies are replaced by adequate and impartial authority.

Here, then, is the high temperature of lawlessness out of which our American Syndicalism directly

springs. The anarchy was increased by the fact that
these labor unions, united in the Federation of Miners,
were openly and aggressively socialistic. Many times
I heard from members their contempt for Mr. Gompers and his Federation of Labor, because he worked
with the employer instead of against him. In Teller
County, I found union cards on which were printed
these words: "Labor produces all wealth. Wealth
belongs to the producer thereof."

There is an ominous significance in these two short
sentences. If the word "labor" were largely interpreted to include all the energy, thought, direction,
ability, and invention that go into the work of mining and its development, the sentence would be innocent enough. But if "labor" is held to mean the
manual service of the wage-earning miner, and that
alone, its meaning may spell disaster. If, as miner,
I am made to believe that I am exclusively the producer of wealth, I shall feel myself defrauded if any
part of it is withheld from me. What I produce and
all that I produce is legitimately my own.

As the I. W. W. comes upon the scene, we are left
in no doubt about their interpretation of these words.
Very active in those mining troubles was one who is
now National Secretary of the I. W. W. It is fair to
let him state his case in his own way. In his pamphlet
explaining the history, structure, and methods [1] he
says, "There is but one bargain the I. W. W. will make
with the employing class—*Complete surrender of all
control of industry to the organized workers.*" These

[1] Published by the I. W. W. Publishing Bureau, New Castle, Pa.
P. O. Drawer 622.

words, which I put in italics, appear in large capital letters in his pamphlet. The other labor master on that occasion is more explicit.

In his *Industrial Socialism*, Mr. Haywood writes:

Long before the coming of the modern Socialist Movement it was understood by the economists that all wealth is produced by labor. How then, it was questioned, can profits be accounted for? If labor produces all wealth why do not the laborers receive their full product? The answer to this question was not known until it came from Karl Marx. Wages, said Marx, are not the full product of labor. Nor are wages any definite part of the product. Wages are simply the selling price of the worker in the market. This selling price, on the average, is just enough to keep the worker in good condition to do his work and produce some one to take his place. For instance, if the worker toils ten hours and produces $10.00 worth of wealth, he does not receive $10.00, nor $5.00. If $2.00 will support him he receives $2.00, and no more. These $2.00 are his wages and the remaining $8.00 are the profits of the capitalist. If the hours of the worker be increased, and better machines introduced, the workers' product is increased, let us say, to $15.00. Do the workers' wages go up? No. They are now but $1.50. The profits, or surplus-value, are now $13.50.

The theory of surplus value is the beginning of all Socialist knowledge. It shows the capitalist in his true light, that of an idler and parasite. It proves to the workers that capitalists should no longer be permitted to take any of their product.

The current publications of this body are full of statements of this same nature, more immature and drastic still. Not alone the capitalist proper, as receiver of interest, is stigmatized as parasite, but employer and "boss" are lumped with the robber class. A mine owner in Cripple Creek, pointing to the words on the union card, said to me: "You see now why they are stealing hundreds of thousands from us every year. They read 'that Labor produces all wealth,' and they take that rogue's gospel straight into the gold mine, stowing away in their clothing the choicest bits of ore, and there is an organized market to buy it. We can't examine them as they come out, as they do in South Africa, or they would leave us in a bunch the first night."

I suggested that the Kaffir thieves in South Africa inclined to pilfering, without any socialistic instruction and that it was charged as confidently where no one had ever heard these phrases.

He held to his point, that the propensity was directly stimulated and justified by this teaching, as indeed the plain logic of it implies. "If they believe what their leaders tell them," he continued, "they are fools *not* to steal it. I would take it in their place, if I thought it belonged to me."

This form of "direct action" in no way characterizes the more instructed Socialism of our time, but it depicts faithfully the opinion of this syndicalist body as it begins to play its part in this country. Even the former editor of the *Brauer-Zeitung*, W. E. Trautmann, now so conspicuous in the fray, writes down calmly:

LABOR THE SOLE PRODUCER

To all the making and development of these social institutions the workers, *and they alone*,[1] contribute their intellect and their manual labor. They have created the instruments to produce wealth with, and improved them as time rolled by.

These institutions are organized in their operative functions to yield profits for a few who never did, nor do, contribute to

[1] The italics are mine.

their making and maintenance, except in a manner to protect
them in the possession of things that they did not make.

In their statement of fundamental principles are
the opening words: "The working class and the employing class have nothing in common." Here is not
even an attempt to distinguish "between employer
and capitalist." Even if the distinction is implied,
the rank and file will not make it. It is the proclaimed
excellence of the movement that its following is from
the ranks of those far down in the social scale; those
excluded from trade unions. Even "the man in the
gutter," is to be taken in as Mr. Haywood insists.
There is much generous-mindedness in this large
brotherhood, but all the more have those who lead it
responsibilities of instruction and explanation. Haywood's ideal organization includes also the working
children and the blacks.[1] How would this general
mass—all the polyglot intermixture of our textile,
mining and iron industries—interpret passages like
those just quoted by their chief instructors? To teach
such as these anything so exhaustively silly as that
manual labor—labor like their own—"produces all
wealth," is so childish as to excite suspicion of its
motive.

If inflammatory appeals like this are really believed
by the leaders, the explanation must lie in the fact
that the birth-pangs of this Colorado strike left emotional hatreds so intense as to make clear thinking or
constructive work impossible. In private conversations, I have found that "labor," as used by leaders,
included far more than the wage earner, but that it

[1] *The General Strike*, p. 13.

was "better not to say much about it." "If we begin
hair-splitting," said one, "we should muddle them
up." "We are out to make them conscious of their
class interests; conscious that those interests are not
the interests of the employers. To make them believe
that and act on it is our work." Another said to me,
"We do just what the preachers and professors do—
we give our people as much light as we think safe,"—
a statement which has its own disconcerting truth
about many others besides preachers and professors.

The shock of this conflict in Colorado had scarcely
ceased before plans were on foot to create a powerful,
all-inclusive labor organization, independent of special
craft unions. Before the year (1904) closed, a gathering was held, resulting in a Secret Conference in
Chicago on the January following. Thirty of the two
and thirty invited delegates were promptly on the
spot. From this came in June the first convention
with its 186 delegates claiming to represent 90,000
members. Only a small part of these proved faithful
to the first declared purpose of the gathering. To
protect themselves from "traitorous intruders," those
first to call the meeting so managed credentials by
shrewd rulings as to prevent the capture of the convention. From that moment the warfare has not
ceased. The National Secretary writes: "It is a fact
that many of those who were present as delegates on
the floor of the first convention and the organizations
that they represented have bitterly fought the I. W.
W. from the close of the first convention to the present
day." For twelve days the principles of the new order

were discussed. The failure and futility of trade union policies got passionate emphasis. In the first form of the Preamble, the most rank offense is that "the trade unions aid the employing class to mislead the workers into the belief that the working class have interests in common with their employers." To avoid this partnership with the enemy, labor in an entire industry must be massed into one common group, no part of which can be pitted by employers against another. This is to be done in such way that all the "members in any one industry, or in all industries, if necessary, cease work whenever there is a strike or lockout in any department thereof, thus making an injury to one an injury to all."

It is to be carefully noted what this means. This all-inclusive union rests upon the assumption that their mass-interests are one and the same, as against the interests of the employing class. As we have seen, this illusion brought troubles thick and fast upon their forerunners, the Knights of Labor. It forced instant differences in this first assembly of the I. W. W. One of the more prominent members, still faithful, as a leading official writes of the Convention:

"All kinds and shades of theories and programs were represented among the delegates and individuals present at the first convention. The principal ones in evidence, however, were four: Parliamentary socialists—two types—impossibilist and opportunist; Marxian and reformist anarchists; industrial unionist; and the labor union fakir. The task of combining these conflicting elements was attempted by the convention."

Their resources were then and there sorely strained to control a membership so diverse in fundamental ideas of social reconstruction.

Of the year that followed before the convention of 1906, Mr. St. John writes as General Secretary:

"The first year of the organization was one of internal struggle for control by these different elements. The two camps of Socialist politicians looked upon the I. W. W. only as a battle ground on which to settle their respective merits and demerits. The Labor fakirs strove to fasten themselves upon the organization that they might continue to exist if the new Union was a success. The anarchist element did not interfere to any great extent in the internal affairs."

Even in the socialist "Western Federation of Miners" irreconcilable differences soon appeared. The Secretary says: "The radical element in the W. F. M. were finally able to force their officials to withdraw their support. The old officials of the I. W. W. then gave up all pretence of having an organization."

A fighting plan was next developed and several "successful" battles fought with the employing class. Their organ, *The Industrial Worker*, was started and the first steps taken toward the defense-fund to save Moyer, Haywood and Pettibone, the jailed officials of the Western Federation. Under the title, "Shall our Brothers be Murdered?" and identifying the issue with the Moyer and Haywood cause with their "basic principle,"—the class struggle, the open propaganda was now fairly under way.

The second convention (1906) brought eighty-three delegates, "representing 60,000 members." A tussle at once began between the "revolutionary camp" and the "reactionaries," whereupon the revolutionists abolished the office of President, putting a revolutionist in the chair. A new executive board was elected and, on adjournment, "the old officials seized the general headquarters, and with the aid of detectives and police held the same, compelling the revolutionists to open up new offices." [1]

The third convention presented no new issue, but the fourth brought a split of more radical character in which we see the "political" pitted squarely against the "industrial socialist." It was this convention which produced the final and amended preamble, sharpening the issues between its own revolutionary method and all the halting processes that wait upon political action. Here the "general strike" of all the members in any industry or "in all industries if necessary" appears as the final resource in its assault on the wage system.

PREAMBLE

The working class and the employing class have nothing in common. There can be no peace so long as hunger and want are found among millions of the working people and the few,

---

[1] In these beginnings, the man of widest popular influence—the "perpetual Socialist candidate" for President, Mr. Debs, was moved to say before a great audience in New York City:

"The revolutionary movement of the working class will date from the year 1905, from the organization of the INDUSTRIAL WORKERS OF THE WORLD. . . . The old form of unionism has long since fulfilled its mission and outlived its usefulness, and the hour has struck for a change."

Mr. Debs has since had his discipline with this body, but he strikes the note of antagonism to the ordinary trade union, of which we have not heard the last.

who make up the employing class, have all the good things of life.

Between these two classes a struggle must go on until the workers of the world organize as a class, take possession of the earth and the machinery of production, and abolish the wage system.

We find that the centering of the management of industries into fewer and fewer hands makes the trade unions unable to cope with the evergrowing power of the employing class. The trade unions foster a state of affairs which allows one set of workers to be pitted against another set of workers in the same industry, thereby helping defeat one another in wage wars. Moreover, the trade unions aid the employing class to mislead the workers into the belief that the working class have interests in common with their employers.

These conditions can be changed and the interest of the working class upheld only by an organization formed in such a way that all its members in any one industry, or in all industries if necessary, cease work whenever a strike or lockout is on in any department thereof, thus making an injury to one an injury to all.

Instead of the conservative motto, "A fair day's wages for a fair day's work," we must inscribe on our banner the revolutionary watchword, "Abolition of the wage system."

It is the historic mission of the working class to do away with capitalism. The army of production must be organized, not only for the every-day struggle with capitalists, but also to carry on production when capitalism shall have been overthrown. By organizing industrially we are forming the structure of the new society within the shell of the old.

It is not easy to exaggerate the importance which members attach to this use of "contracts" and "trade agreements" in defeating strikes.

Scores of warning examples are given in their literature to show how competing unions having contracts of different date are used by employer and

unions alike to defeat "the strike that stands for the
solidarity of labor." W. E. Trautmann thus illustrates the grounds of hostility to trade union policies
in concrete cases which best tell the story.

"The meat wagon drivers of Chicago were organized
in 1902. They made demands for better pay and
shorter hours. Unchecked by any outside influence
they walked out on strike. They had the support of
all other workers in the packing houses. They won.
But before they resumed work the big packing firms
insisted that they enter into a contract. They did.
In that contract the teamsters agreed not to engage
in any sympathetic strike with other employes in the
plants or stockyards. Not only this, but the drivers
also decided to split their union into three. They then
had the 'Bone and Shaving Teamsters,' the 'Packing
House Teamsters,' and the 'Meat Delivery Drivers.'

"Encouraged by the victory of the teamsters, the
other workers in the packing houses then started to
organize. But they were carefully advised not to
organize into one body, or at the best into one National Trades Union. They had to be divided up, so
that the employers could exterminate them all whenever opportunity presented itself.

"Now observe how the dividing-up process worked.
The teamsters were members of the 'International
Union of Teamsters.' The engineers were connected
with the 'International Union of Steam Engineers.'
The firemen, oilers, ashwheelers were organized in the
'Brotherhood of Stationary Firemen.' Carpenters
employed in the stockyards permanently had to join
the 'Brotherhood of Carpenters and Joiners.' The

pipe and steam fitters were members of another 'National Union.' The sausage makers, the packers, the canning department workers, the beef butchers, the cattle butchers, the hog butchers, the bone shavers, etc., each craft group had a separate union. Each union had different rules, all of them not permitting any infringements on them by others. Many of the unions had contracts with the employers. *These contracts expired at different dates.* Most of the contracts contained the clause of "no support to others when engaged in a controversy with the stockyard companies."' [1]

The directory of unions of Chicago shows in 1903, a total of fifty-six different unions in the packing houses, divided up still more in fourteen different national trades unions of the American Federation of Labor.

To relieve this source of trouble, the I. W. W. ask that this collective labor in the meat industry band together into one common union that may act as a unit against employers and "labor fakirs" alike.

In this history of disrupting antagonisms, we watch again the fall of the Knights of Labor. Even the Western Federation of Miners soon refused to pay dues and dropped out to set up again their own local autonomy, thus telling their young offspring that the miners' interests are at least for the present by no means identical with the new and loosely affiliated mass called I. W. W.

Of no less significance is the appearance of another schism, already wider and deeper in Europe, "The *True* I. W. W." This is the "reformist," "anti-

[1] As this goes to press the I. W. W. in New York City attack in the same spirit the "agreements" in the garment makers strike.

violence," and "more moderate" group with headquarters in Detroit. It now sends out its own literature, most of which bears the impress and emphasis
of the "Socialist *Labor* Party," a small but fighting
antagonist of the "Socialist Party." [1]

The older body of the I. W. W. assures us that this
offshoot is "an insignificant faction" which has
"made nothing but mistakes and will continue the
same occupation." The last Convention (the seventh,
1912), in Chicago, has been reported at length by
a derisive member of the smaller but "*True* I. W. W."[2]
He entitles his report the "Bummery Congress" of
the "So-called I. W. W." In the Congress itself pride
was expressed that, in spite of great growth in the
organization, the two enemies, "opportunism" and
"respectability," were effectually excluded. Every
man of them was "red" to the heart, "to a man they
rejected the moral and ethical teaching of the existing
order." They rejoice that negro representatives have
been taken into the brotherhood and that soon "the
whistle will blow for the day when the boss will have
to go to work." At the same time we read in their
report that, "The McNamara brothers, deserted and
repudiated by those for whom they fought and by the
cowardly politicians who sought to make political

---

[1] The differences between the larger and smaller organizations are
clearly stated in a pamphlet by A. Rosenthal entitled, "The Differences between the Socialist Party and the Socialist Labor Party; also
between Socialism, Anarchism, and Anti Political Industrialism."
Printed at 134 Watkins St., Brooklyn, N. Y.

[2] This literature, together with their organ, *The Industrial
Union*, may be had from the General Secretary, H. Richter, P. O.
Box 651, Detroit, Michigan.

capital from their arrest, were not forgotten. When the Secretary Mr. St. John read a stirring message of greeting to them, recognizing them as fighters in the cause of labor and hoping for their early release, it was met with "a shout of approval from the delegates." There is but one thing to be made out of this message. It is not its distinction that it expresses human sympathy with men in distress. Knowing perfectly well what work the McNamaras had done, they are here greeted *for what they have done for "the cause of labor."* Is all that black destruction of life and property really in the "cause of labor"? Yet this, according to the report, "was met with a shout of approval from the delegates."

It is much milder, but still not pleasant reading, that we are to substitute the "General Strike" and the squally passions of public assemblies for court procedure. We read:

The appearance of Bill Haywood Friday morning was the signal for an ovation. In a short address he gave hearty approval to the General Strike proclamation issued by the convention for September 30, and assured the delegates that it would be responded to by a sufficient number of workers in the east to accomplish the release of Ettor and Giovanitti.

In the same tone a French syndicalist reporter now in this country compares the Ettor trial with that of the Haymarket anarchists adding, "Then Haywood gave the authorities a strong warning. A date was set at once for their trial. When it became evident that the world would witness a repetition of the Haymarket incident, another warning reached the court, Ettor and Giovanitti were freed." [1]

[1] *The Independent,* Jan. 9, 1913, p. 79.

VIII

GENERAL CHARACTERISTICS

For our own country, it has considerable significance that the newer immigrant is everywhere conspicuous in the I. W. W. The older American leadership has to consider him in all its tactics. That so many of these new-comers are without votes is no mean asset for revolutionary propaganda.

In the language of English suffragettes, *"Because we have no votes, we must choose other means to gain our ends,"* is an argument I have heard used with the same effect, as the lack of funds in French trade unions is thought to be good reason for direct action. They can neither afford nor wait results of slow and indirect activity.

Of the same nature as a characteristic is the *youth* of the membership. The groups I saw in the West bore this stamp so unmistakably as to suggest bodies of students at the end of a rather jolly picnic. The word "bum" usually applied to them in that region does not fit them. There are plenty of older men, as there are men with every appearance of being "down and out"—with trousers chewed off at the heels, after the manner of tramps, but in face and bearing they are far from "bums."

In one of the speeches the young were addressed as "best material," because they could stand the wear and tear of racking journeys. They were free from family responsibilities, and could at any moment respond to the call of duty. In a report of this year's Convention (1912) "the predominance of young blood" is noted with approval. "Ninety per cent were under thirty years of age," which means a large percentage of very young. But of most importance in this breezy commotion is the extreme and even frantic assertion of its main ideas and practices.

Only a small and unknown fraction of labor in any country has any conscious relation to what is distinctive in Syndicalism, but this defect is more than made up by daring and dramatic assertion of its "principles." These in the main are not new, except in changes wrought by the technical revolution of modern industry. The dream of throwing the labor masses into one all-embracing Union is at least as old as the "Grand National Consolidated Trade Unions" of 1834, with the addition, moreover, of the "General Strike" as its great weapon. We have seen how much of Syndicalism was a propelling force in the meteoric career of the Knights of Labor. As this streak of fire burned out in the early nineties, Syndicalism reappears in France. It appears in action, in metaphysical quiddities, and in literary rhapsodies. In action, it rebels against the halting ineffectiveness of legislative reforms in cities and government. It is noted that every law and ordinance to improve things socially has to be amended year after year before it works at all, and even then, it works but lamely for the general good. Against these discouragements, the more fiery and headlong spirits among Socialists rebel and intellectually fraternize with anarchists. They rebel against the State (as anarchists always have) and against its lumbering procedure through parliamentary delays. These social laws, says one of them, "are mere substitutes for action. They move with feet of lead when we want wings." To fly to their goal instead of walking to it, becomes a passion. As they turn gruffly from the State and from the lazy ways of legal change, they also turn from the employer. This is among the drolleries of the situation. After employers have been revelling in their own refusal to "recognize" trade unions, our I. W. W. turn the tables. "We, too, refuse to 'recognize' employers." "We quit work without consulting them. We go back to work without notice. In all ways they shall be ignored."

If capitalism is "organized corruption," why should labor, the "all-creative," recognize it? This, too, it is said is as insincere and farcical as to recognize the politician and the state. This impatient activity was all there before it got philosophic expression in the writings of George Sorel. He gave to it the metaphysical touch that works as mystically on the imagination as the shadowy dialectic of Marx worked upon the awed devotees who could but faintly guess his meaning.

Rapidly a group of writers, either workingmen or in the closest way identified with them, put the new purpose into a literature for propaganda. If there is no help from the State, the politician, or the employer, the logic is evident. The worker must turn to himself and to the trade union as his fighting arm. If the State and employer alike are the enemy, this enemy must be disabled, in all ways badgered and discomfited. As all the workers are to be brought in, the lowest possible dues must be charged or even no dues at all. The strike then becomes supreme. It must be short, sharp and unexpected. It must be sudden and explosive to show its power. It must aim at the most vital spot. For *practice*, you may keep your hand in by strikes in smaller industries, but transportation is the great target,—the railroad best of all, because it is the nerve system of distribution. Cripple this, and hunger will stalk the streets within a fortnight. Always, too, sabotage is in order. It frets and harries the employer. It strikes at his profits. With skill and a "fine conspiracy" among the laborers, the spoiled product cannot be traced. The destroyer may work as subtly as a disease with no fear of punishment.

This gospel of destruction has a quite fascinating versatility. On the one hand we are assured that capitalism has reached senility. Though never more prolific of depravity, never more active in parasitic lecheries, its real power is so near its end, that a few years of adroit and vigorous assault and it will tumble of its own weight.

Others speak as if the strength of capitalism was never so great. The proof offered is that three generations of social and other legislation meant to curb its power have obviously failed.

The supposed discovery of this failure of political and social reform is vital. If these attempts have done nothing to relieve the exploitation of the weak: if reform does not even show a tendency to such alleviation then sedition may justify itself.

It is the essence of "social legislation" that it stands for the public welfare and not for any special interest. Piece by piece, since 1802, in England, it has been built up. It has tried to "regulate" the more lawless forces of competing private interests, as well as the health, housing, hours and conditions of labor, the child in industry, occupational diseases, industrial insurance, and then, with more specific intent, the direct curbing of corporate powers in banks, railways, insurance, and the whole extending network of big business as it becomes national in its affiliations. It is generally believed that these forces have been restrained to the common good; that they cannot, as of old, show contempt for public opinion, even if they feel it. Large sections of English, German and French Socialists agree in this, that legislative reforms have already produced immense benefits and that the way, *even for Socialists*, is along this same pathway of enlarged and more coherent amelioration.

True or false this issue cuts to the marrow of our question. It presents the case about which the main struggle of the future is to turn. Is the present society to be "reformed" into some tolerable measure of justice and "equal hope for all"? Are the main lines of this regeneration already traced, with such clearness that we have only to continue as we have begun? Or, are we to confess their futility and fall to, in good I. W. W. fashion, to ridicule charities, philanthropies, social settlements, welfare work, sliding scales, arbitration and the full score of other attempts to unite and organize the entire good will of society and not merely a "class conscious" part of it?

But syndicalist criticism goes much further. We have, for example, taken the Post Office away from the private profit maker to manage it democratically and directly for public uses. Most of the world's railroads have been taken by the State; a large part of trolley lines, gas, telephone, telegraph; a good deal of private insurance, mines and water powers, together with a long list of municipal hotels, restaurants, milk, supplies; all these have already been "socialized," "taken over" for public administration "in the interests of all." These are for the most part imperfectly managed, but their intent is socialistic, because they lessen the area of private investment. Are we to continue in this direction by carrying out this same process to its supposed logical completeness? When it is applied to banks, land, shipping, mills, mines, and the entire body of more important industries, shall we have the essentials of the Socialist State?

In every advanced country, this is the express claim of a most influential part of the active and disciplined leadership among Socialists. At the points where they secure political power and responsibility, this opinion steadily gains in influence. This view assumes that the evils of capitalism are slowly being lessened and that the way to diminish them further still, is to extend the whole regulating and "socializing" process now under way.

The hot protest against the above is not confined to the I. W. W. Hosts of more revolutionary spirits reject these "bourgeois conciliations," but none reject them with more contemptuous unanimity than Syndicalists in general. They tell us that our prevailing business system never was more triumphant or unrepentant. Never did it strip labor closer to the bone. Never did it lug away to private vaults so large a share of that wealth wrung from the toil and sweat of those who labor. From its inner kingdom of finance, its cunning devices of "underwriting" and control of credit, marketing securities, over-capitalization, and such like juggleries, the powers of capitalism so control the final dividing of products as to get absolutely and relatively an increasing pillage for their share. In these round terms of condemnation Syndicalists speak to us of discredited social and economic reform alike. It has no more fundamental characteristic than this.

No man believing this could escape the syndicalist logic. If for nearly three generations, all the stupendous energies to curb the competitive spirit working through capitalism, have come to nothing; if these energies, working through local and parliamentary activities have left us relatively more enfeebled than ever before the tyrannies of private capital, why should further appeal to politics and "reforms" inspire a spark of hope?

Syndicalism represents this "army of the disillusioned." As one of them writes—"In good faith we asked elected officials to get redress through new laws only to find that, one by one, each spouting coward lost himself body and soul to the real interests of the proletariat. When we had seen John Burns, Miller-and, Viviani Briand and scores of lesser socialist officials yield to the tawdry fopperies of bourgeois entertainers and official ceremonies, we got onto that game. Now we know where to look. What is to be done will be done directly by ourselves, the working class, and we will forge the weapons to do it."

This bitterness of disappointment had wide expression in France before any "philosopher" (Sorel, Berth, Lagardelle or the supposed succor of Professor Henri Bergson) had given it more oracular expression. In the United States it is the same. Several years before our "intellectuals" furnished a literary ritual to the I. W. W., hundreds of soap-box evangelists had been telling their listeners to turn their backs both upon political reform and upon the whole "scavenger brood of trade union cormorants." "Until the working class turns to itself, every day is lost." As these disappointments gain in volume, literary organs, East and West, spring up to give them voice. From men of university training, we hear that "the proletariat is losing ground actually and relatively." "Against labor, capitalism is more and more holding its own." It grows more and more powerful. It does this because it has affiliations, economic and political, which give it such strategic pliancy that it can shift its ground, adapt itself to hostile legislation, to trade unions—which it honestly thinks a scourge and a nuisance; to costly welfare adjuncts, even to city and state ownership, without losing an atom of its essential dominance.

Mr. English Walling's able book *Socialism As It Is*, is filled with convictions and evidence on this point. When Col. Roosevelt gave out his program at Chicago (August, 1912), it was attacked from many quarters as "Socialistic." Socialist papers twitted him with stealing their thunder. The Nationalist Organ at Washington paralleled the Socialist and the new Roosevelt platforms to prove what valuable plunder the colonel had stolen from their camp. Yet Mr. Walling finds no item in Mr. Roosevelt's list that is in any intelligible sense socialistic. He writes:

Mr. Roosevelt's programme is, in the Socialist view, neither populistic nor socialistic *in the slightest degree*, but capitalistic. He has not appropriated a single Socialist demand. He has merely taken up certain measures the Socialists took from other radicals. These measures were placed on our programme because it was seen that they were capable of immediate realization, because though previously neglected, they might be accepted by the majority of capitalists without any loss to themselves or any necessary danger to the capitalist system.

To this the "National Socialist" replies through Mr. Ghent: "Mr. Walling would have come somewhat nearer the facts by saying just the opposite of what he here asserts. It is ridiculous to maintain that Roosevelt's programme is in no degree Socialistic." The editorial raises the great shade of Marx himself, who says that these reform measures "are unavoidable as a means of entirely revolutionizing the mode of production." (August 24, 1912.)

The issue here seems to me obviously against Mr. Walling and those who hold with him. It is "ridiculous to maintain that Roosevelt's programme is in *no degree* Socialistic." The whole syndicalist flouting of "reforms" and the service they have performed, and are likely to perform, is, I think, just as obviously a mistaken view, but its emphasis is a hall-mark of Syndicalism. Its ideas became heady and extreme, they pass, as if caught in rapids that cannot be stemmed, to the most revolutionary limit, as "Class *Consciousness*" for example passes into "Class *War*." Our own labor history is here illuminating.

As the Knights of Labor began to totter and the Federation of Labor took shape, the extremists of the "class-war" type formed the "Socialist Trade and Labor Alliance," pitted both against the Federation of Labor and the Knights of Labor. Every difference, every enmity toward the employing class and toward unionism " pure and simple " got more thumping emphasis.

In its later stages, the Knights of Labor were swept by this more revolutionary emotion. This temper has now passed to an order with another lettering—the I. W. W. It has much of the liturgy of the Knights of Labor; much of its more indiscriminate working-class inclusiveness. It has also much of which the Knights of Labor consciously knew little. This consists chiefly in sharpening the fighting edge of every revolutionary weapon in the socialist armory. An hundred Knights of Labor strikes practised *sabotage*, but they knew not the word, much less had they any philosophy about it. The new warfare has passed the fig-leaf innocencies and consciously clothes itself in pragmatic habits. It has its metaphysic and chooses for expositor, one of the most brilliant among modern philosophers who is thought to dignify and sanction our simpler and more direct activities. No less fateful is it that Syndicalism comes among us at a time when the general atmosphere is electric with rude and querulous discontent; when censure of our main stabilities, constitutions, courts, judges, will bring applause in any general audience in the United States. This criticism of our "secular sanctities" is not in the least an affair of mobs alone. It speaks openly and unashamed in the books and utterances of scholars and first rate publicists. In nearly three hundred regular socialist periodicals, this defiant criticism has become the habitual reading of some millions of our inhabitants. I have heard a large working-class audience burst into uproarious guffaws at this sentence spoken from the platform: "No society could exist that did not respect its courts of justice." A very able university President recently attempted the defense of our conserving institutions in a popular arena. He was so heckled and worsted that he left the meeting, feeling, as he told me, that "they thoroughly wiped the floor with me."

Any one who thinks these illustrations carry any exaggeration has only to spend some hours on a bundle of this literature which he may buy on the streets in any industrial center of the United States. The lengths to which this challenging goes may be seen in an incident two months ago in a western town. The judge, as he passed sentence for "conspiracy," had spoken gravely of what a court of justice signifies. He allowed the condemned man "a few words in his own behalf," and listened, apparently not much disturbed, to the following:

There are only a few words that I care to say, and this court will not mistake them for a legal argument, for I am not acquainted with the phraseology of the bar; nor the language common to the courtroom.

There are two points which I want to touch upon—the indictment itself and the misstatement of the prosecuting attorney. The indictment reads: "The People of the State of California against J. W. Whyte and others." It's a hideous lie. The people in this courtroom know that it is a lie; the court itself knows that it is a lie, and I know that it is a lie. . . . You cowards throw the blame upon the people, but I know who is to blame and I name them—it is Spreckels and his partners in business and this court is the lackey and lickspittle of that class, defending the property of that class against the advancing horde of starving American workers.

The prosecuting attorney in his plea to the jury accused me of saying on a public platform at a public meeting: "To hell with the courts; we know what justice is." He told a great truth when he lied, for if he had searched the innermost recesses of my mind he could have found that thought, never expressed by me before, but which I express now. "To hell with your courts, I know what justice is," for I have sat in your courtroom day after day and have seen members of my class pass before this, the so-called bar of justice. . . .

I have seen you, Judge ————, and others of your kind, send them to prison because they dared to infringe upon the sacred rights of property. You have become blind and deaf to the rights of man to pursue life and happiness, and you have crushed those rights so that the sacred rights of property should be preserved. Then you tell me to respect the law. I don't. I did violate the law, and I will violate every one of your laws and still come before you and say: "To hell with the courts," because I believe that my right to live is far more sacred than the sacred right of property that you and your kind so ably defend.

I don't tell you this with the expectation of getting justice, but to show my contempt for the whole machinery of law and justice as represented by this and every other court. The prosecutor lied, but I will accept it as a truth and say again so that you, Judge ————, may not be mistaken as to my attitude: "To hell with your courts; I know what justice is."

This speech has made a hero of the jailed Syndicalist. When his confinement ends, as a vendor of "hot stuff," his place upon the I. W. W. platforms will be secure.

To see the I. W. W. as it is; to see it with the eye that understands, whether forgivingly or in condemnation, is to see it as the child of strife. It is born out of conflict. The terrible struggle of the American Railway Union in and about Chicago which made Mr. Debs so famous, has the initial characteristic of Syndicalism becoming conscious of itself. The fight was so desperate that all the unions in the industry were thrown together. This gave that elated sense of collective force, out of which this revolutionary impulse springs. In saying that the I. W. W. began in the Colorado strike, means only that a more concentrated contest added enough intensity to the feeling of labor solidarity to make it more conscious of a new power. Mr. Debs' education in his own strike prepared him for the first I. W. W. Convention a few months later as effectively as if he had been among the miners. The most influential men in that Chicago gathering (1905) had had stormy and bitter experience.

It is this war-origin of the I. W. W. which is its weakness on the constructive side. That it is a child of strife, brings back upon itself the very qualities which are admirable for battle, but which make stability and organization impossible. They lead to the quarrels which disrupt the attempts at steady team work from the very start. The practical danger to the I. W. W. is absence of trouble. If industry were so organized as to prevent strikes, the I. W. W. would disappear.

In 1909, came the outbreak at McKees Rocks, with dictatorial mismanagement at the top which brought from some of our most capitalistic papers the most caustic censure. This high and mighty tone was the very breath of life to the I. W. W. Flocking from every quarter, it brought sympathizers ready to fight in their cause. It is this fighting feature which attracts so many journalists and those of artistic and literary temperament. It is an impulse so rich in dramatic satisfactions as to be the happiest windfall for their mood.

All the drudgeries and enduring strain demanded by reforms like civil service, good housing, social hygiene, insurance, and the like, are wan and colorless compared to the inscrutable pageantry—all the unexpectedness and mystery of an I. W. W. attack.

In its whole popular theory, as well as in the field-work of its practice, it has the same revolutionary emphasis which must be considered under successive heads.

IX

THE WAR OF THE CLASSES

AMONG syndicalist "fundamentals" is the clear division of our society into the tool-owning capitalist class, on the one side, and the wage receiving class on the other. These confront each other as enemies. The employing class is entrenched behind citadels of private property; behind the whole stupendous mechanism of production, behind the Constitution, the courts, and all that "law and order" mean when interpreted and enforced by the possessing classes. Here, massed in fancied security, is the foe of labor. Without, is the vast, ill-organized multitude of the workers, stupefied and confused by religious and secular instruction guided in the interest of those behind the fortress. The task of Syndicalism is to wake this formless mob of dupes out of its stupor; to make them see the enemy as he is, and to see himself the victim, purposely shut out and excluded from the feasting trenchers behind the walls. Between this guarded minority and the huge, straggling multitude on the outside there is as little in common as between the robber and the robbed. With these beliefs, Syndicalists ask, how is this formless multitude to be brought to its senses? How make it see the ugly facts of its own enslavement?

For this, the propaganda of the I. W. W. exists. Its teeming literature bristles with metaphors, caricatures, exhortations,—all with the single aim of forcing this overtopping majority to look searchingly into the gulf that yawns between it and the enemy. Syndicalism marks its progress by the number of its conversions. Trautmann's pamphlet, *Industrial Unionism*, opens with the words:

"A portion of the workers, in ever-increasing numbers, recognize the fact that the working class and the employing class have nothing in common, and that the struggle must go on until all the toilers come together and take and hold that which they produce by their labor. The workers begin to see that they must not only prepare themselves to hold their own against the aggressions of their oppressors, but also destroy the fortifications behind which the enemy has entrenched himself in his possessions of land, mills, mines and factories. What is of benefit to the employers must, self-evidently, be detrimental to the employes."

This doctrine is not peculiar to Syndicalism. The general socialist movement knows it of old and has laid upon it all manner of emphasis.

A very powerful section of Socialism, however, has learned some restraint in the uses of class antagonism as embodied in this doctrine. Many of the ablest advocates of Socialism have declared themselves wholly against it. A dozen able men could be quoted to this effect. H. G. Wells writes sentences like these: "Modern Socialism has cleared itself of that jealous hatred of prosperity that was once a part of class-war Socialism." "It refuses no one who will serve it. It is no narrow doctrinaire cult. It does not seek the best of an argument, but the best of a world. Its worst enemies are those foolish and litigious advocates who antagonize and estrange every development of human Good Will and does not pay tribute to their vanity in open acquiescence. Its most loyal servants, its most effectual helpers on the side of art, invention and public organization and political reconstruction, may be men who will never adopt the Socialist name."[1] It is from a leader of the English Parliamentary Socialists that we have this opinion: "It is the whole of society and not merely a part of society that is developing toward Socialism. The consistent exponent of the class struggle must, of course, repudiate these doctrines, but then the class struggle is far more akin to Radicalism than to Socialism." "Socialists should, therefore, think of the State and of political authority not as the expression of majority rule or of the will of any section, but as the embodiment of the life of the whole community."[2]

A clear-headed Socialist like Mr. W. J. Ghent stands stiffly for the class struggle which he rightly derives from the "economic interpretation of history," but he sounds a warning to those who overdo it. He admits that the "intellectuals" outside the proletariat devised and gave this very doctrine, "the philosophy of it and the reasons for it," to the manual workers. He then adds,[3] "It needs to be said plainly that there is no more shameless misleader of the Socialist proletariat than the demagogue who tries to create antagonism against the educated men in the movement."

[1] *New Worlds for Old*, pp. 321–307.
[2] Macdonald's *Socialism and Government*, Vol. I, p. 91.
[3] *Socialism and Success*, p. 164.

This same attack on "intellectuals" is incessant in the I. W. W. It appears in more popular form in the Italian Syndicalist, Enrico Leone; so too, the German Syndicalist, "Der Pionier," taunts the socialist members of the Reichstag with being anything and everything except wage earners. "How, it asks, can they lead those of whose lives they know nothing?"

It is wholly true that this class conscious appeal has in it most indispensable utilities. The workers must be made conscious of every whit of common interest which is genuinely their own. This consciousness of "unified labor interests" has in it great educational value. Its value is all the more precious because the limits of its actual realization are so narrow. It should be encouraged and tolerated because the little it can do has such merit. The more labor *feels* its brotherhood, the more power it possesses to enlarge its strategic opportunities. Socialism does well to make the most of it. It has great kindling and arousing power. It is true too that the main struggle has to be their own. In this, they are now prepared to take advice so long dealt out to them. It is a classic illustration of "bourgeois morals" to encourage self-reliance; to teach the poor and the humble to "help themselves;" to trust to their own inner resources rather than yield in flabby acquiescence to their more fortunate brothers.

Upon reflection, the wage earners conclude that this well-meant counsel is excellent in spite of its suspicious origin. They propose now to "help themselves." In order to make the advice serviceable, they are to take it not as individuals, but all together. They are to have "collective efficiency, in helping themselves." To be sure, this mass-method does not lend itself to the convenience of the superior class as in the older ways of charity, but self-reliance may be the gainer.

The fervors that bring great masses of labor together, quenching for the time all pettiness and bickering, consuming mean enmities among leaders, are priceless. By the help of this deepened "class consciousness" trade unionism in the world has built itself into a tower of strength. It has made "collective bargaining" possible. It is this enlarged and quickened sense of brotherhood that has won every memorable strike in history, like that of the London dockers of 1886, and that of our miners in 1903. It is the same uplifting that has won the political triumphs of completer suffrage (as in Austria and Belgium) against the "vote of property."

It is difficult to state too strongly the strategic and informing value of the class-conscious appeal, for immediate and practical purposes. But this is not all the story. To pass from these conceded uses to the idea of a "class struggle," over-stimulated and enforced as an unflinching principle, in the manner of the I. W. W., has in it the logic of social dissolution. From long and hard experience, some of the ablest men that Socialism has produced no longer make this mistake. They have learned a far larger thought of interests that infold not "labor" alone, but the whole stumbling, yet climbing race of men and women in the world. They have learned that "interests" bind us up and down, perpendicularly as well as horizontally. The claim that interests unite the wage earners alone and apart from all others, leads to the most treacherous morass through which they stagger to their goal. Labor has depths of interests that are in common, but far greater depths of interest that are *human and all-inclusive.*

Socialism has half learned this lesson. Syndicalism apparently has it yet to learn. From the beginnings, Socialism has had its spasms of working-class exclusiveness, but its strength and progress can be definitely marked by its hospitable working fellowship with men of other and larger training or at least different training. Syndicalism if it lives can have no other history.[1]

This sharpening of antagonisms leads not only to warfare against "intellectuals but just as inevitably to warfare of the unskilled against the more skilled worker thus bringing on the conflict within the wage-earning group.

In ominous words **with his** italics Mr. Walling writes: [2]

"This mass of workers, it now appears, will no longer wait for the permission or the co-operation of the skilled before they strike, *and this constitutes nothing less than a revolution in the*

[1] The following is a recent "field note."

"St. Louis Industrialists have organized branches 'prohibiting lawyers, preachers and professional parasites and grafters from membership.' We believe there are several such branches, but Branch 1 will not accept a member who is not industrially employed. Branch 2 is non-dues paying. Evidently these comrades want to make it as easy as possible for actual workers to join. The purpose of these Industrialist Branches is to teach Socialism and industrial organization at one and the same time. Branch 1 does not use dues stamps."

[2] *New Review,* Jan. 18, 1912.

labor movement. If the aristocracy of labor will give them no consideration, they are ready, if necessary, to fight the aristocracy. *It is this warfare between the skilled and the unskilled and not any other difference of principle, that constitutes the essence of all the labor union and socialist attacks on the I. W. W."*

From the first meeting between Sorel and Pelloutier to the present day, "intellectuals" have been of such indispensable service to the cause, that no intelligible account of it could be given without them. It is one of the signs of democratic and revolutionary change that men of rare intellectual gift show, like Tolstoi, a passion to identify themselves with the humblest of their kind. Some of the most scorching passages against intellectuals, masquerading as genuine folk of the fourth estate, are by men who are themselves nothing if not "intellectuals." No one can surpass M. Sorel himself in this. Bernard Shaw could not do it better. In his *L'avenir Socialiste des Syndicats,* Sorel has only a withering contempt for the educated interlopers in the movement. Their superiorities, he says, are among the superstitions of the proletariat. Like mountebanks, the intellectuals exploit this superstition, flaunt their degrees and "professional humbug" before simple men not yet free from illusions on which pedants have always fattened. To get simple minded working people free from this strutting despotism and from all the benumbing "authority" for which it stands, is one of the greater aims of Syndicalism. Among the emblazonries borne in the recent I. W. W. parade at Lawrence one read, "No God, no Master." These words are a perfect echo of Sorel's thought. There should be no "mastery," but self-mastery. Neither God nor man should supervise, order, or interfere. This is the fight also against those who claim more enlightenment than their fellows.

Sorel's dudgeon against the "intellectual" is that (as intellectual) he is always on the hunt for power over men. This leads the superior person to the political field where, among the suavities of parliamentary etiquette, his slow but certain corruption begins. In order to climb higher still he sells out to the next higher stratum of respectability. The politician, as Sorel portrays him, is the exact counterpart of the prostitute:—a creature for sale. He is forever trying to persuade labor that its real interests are the same as his own, or of the party to which he adds luster. The whole mercenary pack is "*avide de posseder les profits des emplois public.*" [1]

The reply to this smart persiflage, is that it skips all the facts. In every advanced nation labor has made its own solid and incontestable gains in alliance with political intellectuals who have given every proof of sincerity that disinterested life-long service carries.

It must be conceded that the most sacred struggle in the world is that in which labor may be said to lead;—the struggle toward a regenerated and reorganized society in which at last every rotten shred of unfair privilege shall be cut out. But this highest and hardest task is not to be performed by one class alone. Not one in the great total of us all who has good will shall be shut out of it. All who can and will, must play their part. Yes, even the defamed possessor of over-weighted millions, if he is led to look

[1] See *La Decomposition du Marxism.*

out on the great scene from some higher place, shall have a welcome. As the "Noble Knights" grew uneasy and ashamed because physicians were excluded from their own elect, so our revolutionary brothers, the I. W. W., will learn the shallowness of railing as they now do against the "intellectuals" because they "are not of us."

The struggle toward the larger life to which the world's good will is committed is a task too heavy and too sacred to be borne and shared alone by any "class." It will forever remain a *human* task, from which no soul shall be shut out who wills to help.

X

THE GENERAL STRIKE

As things are felt and lived before any literary skill gives them form, there were plenty of incoherent uprisings with every characteristic of the General Strike, generations before Sorel's sombre genius turned them into a religion for mass-activity. It is the despised "intellectuals," now and in the past, who have furnished the effective formulas for the General Strike; as they adjusted the conception to present proletarian uses; as in the middle of the last century, one of the most brilliant journalists of Europe, Emile de Giradin, conceived of it as the one weapon against the third Napoleon. In Victor Hugo's *Histoire d'un Crime*, in twenty lines that burn like a flame, the technique of the General Strike is given. He uses the very words "La Grève Universelle." The very term "folding the arms" (croisant les bras), which I have heard from I. W. W. orators, occurs in the passage. The poet appeals to society to create a "great emptiness" round this would-be despot, by cutting him off through the general boycott from every source of help. The picture is the more complete because a man famous in later days, Jules Favre, argued successfully in opposition by setting forth the same practical difficulties that have crippled most subsequent application of the General Strike, except for narrower and less ambitious ends.

Revolutionary spirits for half a century have speculated upon the strike and the logic to which it leads.
An Egyptian scholar tells me he could make a book
on strikes in Ancient Egypt. It is one of the oldest
weapons with which labor has tried to defend itself
against demands or conditions no longer felt to be
endurable. It still has uses sacred as liberty, but
never was this strong-sword so costly or so dangerous;
never did it require higher skill and caution to wield
it wisely than it does today.

The guild-life of the Middle Ages was filled with
strikes. Like a shadow they followed the whole history of the trade union through the eighteenth and
nineteenth centuries, nor were they by any means
confined to labor organizations. Organization gave
them a dreaded power with which employer and the
law have to reckon.

The danger of the strike has increased (especially
for those who use it) with every tightening of the social
and industrial organism.[1]

Syndicalism revives the strike and seeks a new
significance in the logic of this labor agency. If a little
strike brings some bit of industry to a standstill and
a large sympathetic strike paralyzes a lot of industries,
is it not obvious that the "strike-universal" would
stop every wheel and every productive activity in the
world's workshop? It would be as effective as Tolstoi's cry to the millions of his countrymen—"just
stop paying taxes—all of you together—and Government is at an end." If "all together" they would re-

---

[1] Some one should do for industrial warfare what Norman Angel
has done for war between nations, in "The Great Illusion."

fuse and also refuse to enlist as soldiers, the unwieldy, creaking mechanism of the State grows silent.

The only trouble with the remedy is the "all-together." This has been the perplexity of the general strike: first, to get the ear of labor, and then—harder still—to get common and consenting action. For a third of a century what has been called by Mr. Ettor "the high tribunal of our comrades," "general strikes" have taken place. Especially in our American syndicalist literature, the European risings are given the glamor of "success" partly because they are so far away that almost any assertion may be made about them. For example, Mr. Haywood calls the French Commune of 1871 "the greatest general strike known in modern times." He says the proletariat would have won this "greatest general strike" if it had not been for France and Germany, which is like saying the South would have beaten in the Civil War if it had not been for the North. In the Province of Alicante, Spain, almost forty years ago, a branch of the "international" created a general strike with syndicalist intent, not of raising wages but expressly to "remake a society in which free men could live." This was rather ruthlessly put down by the troops, but Mr. Haywood says it "won" nevertheless.

The Swedish strike and the greater ones in Russia, he puts down among the "successes." In France, he watched the recent syndicalist strike on the railroads and thus describes it:[1] "This is the way it worked—and I tell it to you in hopes that you will spread the good news to your fellow-workers and apply it your-

[1] *The General Strike*, W. A. Haywood, p. 9.

selves whenever occasion demands—*namely*, that of
making the *capitalist suffer*. Now there is only one
way to do that; that is, to strike him in the place where
he carries his heart and soul, his center of feeling—the
pocketbook. And that is what those strikers did.
They began at once to make the railroads lose money,
to make the government lose money, to make transportation a farce so far as France was concerned.
Before I left that country, on my first visit—and it
was during the time that the strike was on—there were
50,000 tons of freight piled up at Havre, and a propor-
tionately large amount at every other seaport town.
This freight the railroaders would not move. They
did not move at first, and when they did it was in this
way: they would load a trainload of freight for Paris
and by some mistake it would be billed through to
Lyons, and when the freight was found at Lyons,
instead of being sent to the consignee at Paris it was
carried straight through the town on to Bayonne or
Marseilles or some other place—to any place but
where it properly belonged. Perishable freight was
taken out by the trainload and sidetracked." This is
thought to have added value because of its illustrative
details. It offers practical suggestions that may serve
as models to the younger pupils of the I. W. W. The
event in France was very bracing to Mr. Haywood.
"That," he says, "is certainly one splendid example
of what the general strike can accomplish for the
working class."

Much use is made of the strike on the Italian
railways as specially informing because the employes had but one union card,—stenographers,

train dispatchers, freight handlers, train crews, and the section crews. "Every one who works on the railroad is a member of the organization." Here, no separate union can be kept at work while others go out. No employer's contract with one union can be enforced while other unions are on strike. Though there are "thirty-seven trades," they can all act as a single unit.

It was this precaution that gave such advantage to his own Western Federation of Miners in its armed tilts with capital. He says of it: "Everyone employed in and around the mines belongs to the same organization; where, when we went on strike, the mine closed down. They thought that was a very excellent system. So the strike was declared. They at once notified the engine winders, who had a separate contract with the mine owners, that they would not be allowed to work. The engine winders passed a resolution saying that they would not work. The haulers took the same position. No one was allowed to approach the mines to run the machinery. Well, the mine manager, like mine managers everywhere, taking unto himself the idea that the mines belonged to him, said, 'Certainly the men won't interfere with us. We will go up and run the machinery.' And they took along the office force. But the miners had a different notion and they said, 'You can work in the office, but you can't run this machinery. That isn't your work. If you run that you will be scabbing; and we don't permit you to scab—not in this section of the country, now.'" He then states his ideal— "One great organization—big enough to take in the black man, the white man; big enough to take in all nationalities—an organization that will be strong enough to obliterate state boundaries, to obliterate national boundaries, and one that will become the great industrial force of the working class of the world."

This is the ritualistic formula from which Syndicalism draws its highest moral allegiance and it is not to be met by scoffing or by stalwart platitudes. It has brought to the movement an eager host of disciples aching to give themselves utterly to some ennobling human service.

If this together-impulse were wisely nurtured; if it could be freed from reckless and destructive suggestion; if it could be given organic restraint, its service would be great.

I have watched for hours throngs of men and women under the spell of this appeal to strike *together*. Packed close were a dozen nationalities requiring five or six interpreters. Stentorially, the thing had to be said and resaid until the message was a common possession. It was always a message which for the hour obliterated every distinction of race. "There are no Poles, no Greeks, neither Jew nor Italian here, but only brothers" is the unwearying exhortation.

There is in this fusion an immediate ethical power over generous spirits, the results of which one meets everywhere in the United States. I have many times asked young men and women what first caught their interest. From the best of them, it is invariably this— "Nothing has yet done for labor at the bottom. Where it is helpless, ignorant, without speech, it has been neglected and abused. It is pushed into every back alley and into all work that is hardest and most dangerous. Society forgets it. The trade unions that should befriend it forget it too. Now comes the I. W. W. with the first bold and brotherly cry which these ignored masses have ever heard."

With no fussy qualifications, this must be granted to the I. W. W. No violence of speech or deed can honorably deprive them of this stirring element in their entreaty. As will be shown later, it is with this that we must learn to coöperate or fail miserably in social duty, and in the best uses of our social experience.

It is again only when we recognize this saving element in the propaganda that we can understand why leaders succeed in making a kind of religion of the general strike. It is because they connect it by intimate association with this over-arching thought of a world brotherhood. As intimately, too, they connect it with the world's waking desire to stop the consenting butcheries of war. Nowhere can we read more uplifting passages against these inhumanities than in syndicalist literature and in the possibility that international brotherhoods of labor may sometime so universally lay down their tools before the threat of war, as to startle the world into some great action against the war infamy.

All this is beyond and above criticism, but these fair dreams are not peculiar to I. W. W. They are shared by millions who bear other names.

Our practical concern is also and largely with things prosaic: with the ways and means through which we are to get possession of the new and regenerated world. Hundreds of differing methods are thrust upon

us for choice and therefore for criticism. It is not
merely the general strike, it is even more the manner
and spirit of its application.

At a socialist congress in 1891, great enthusiasm was
roused by a resolution against the criminal stupidity
of war as a means of settling disputes. A Dutch
clergyman of great influence was the proposer. "Let
us meet the first declaration of war by a general
strike," was its purport. Let the workers of the
world answer to a man by quietly laying down their
tools. Let them reply to the great malefactors, "We
work no longer to waste labor and human life, we will
only work to save labor and to lengthen and enrich
life."

One may gladly believe that somewhere beyond us,
a strike may become holy in such a cause. But it is
not this with which our average I. W. W. proposals
have to do. The strike energy is urged to exercise
itself at the heart of our economic activity for a
specific purpose. It is not first for political advantages. It is the exclusive economic emphasis which
makes the general strike a club for Anarchists rather
than for Socialists. Many older Socialists favored the
general strike for political ends, while they considered the general economic strike ridiculous. In the
pamphlet just quoted the whole idea is that of the
Syndicalist. Labor, it says, has now actually got the
machinery of production in its own hands. It has
only to educate itself to take it and run it. "Only
make labor conscious of its possession and the battle
is ours." There is a collection of syndicalist opinions
on the general strike that appeared in their most im-

portant organ, the "Mouvement Socialiste." [1] The entire object is to make labor clearly conscious of its relation to economic power. Wage earners are to be made first to believe it has this power and then to act upon the belief. "The revolution is to be first in the thought, and then in act." To popularize these conceptions is the work of their propaganda. Throughout is the "catastrophic idea."

As many of the revolutionary spirits in Europe and among English Chartists in the days before 1848 were inflamed with hopes of some impending political change, those of this temper are now caught up by beliefs that an economic revolution is at hand. The centralizing forces of present day industry open a new vista to these believers. "We have not now," they tell us, "to worry over the practical difficulties of the 'strike-universal.' We can turn a partial strike into one that has unusual results. To stop transportation alone is to stop a thousand other industries." "With a motion of the hand," says Pataud, "I can make Paris dark as night." It is these mechanical possibilities which have transformed the tactics of "this last great remedy," as a little knowledge of chemistry may give new terrors to sabotage.

This has been the strategy of recent strikes of this character. But—what the believers do not tell us, it has also been the source of their failure. Like Mr. Haywood, Arnold Roller's study of the General Strike turns an indiscriminate mass of historic revolts

---

[1] These opinions are now found in a small volume, *La Grève Générale et le Socialisme*. See also *L'Action Syndicaliste*, Griffuelhes, pp. 27–37.

into instructive material from which labor is to learn
its lessons. The Spanish strike in Alcoy in 1874 was
not for any added pittance to the wage, but for "the
construction of a free society." To be sure, it was at
once put down by the troops but it is a part of the
great pageant of reconstruction.[1]

Our American strike for eight hours in 1886 is
noticed because politics was ignored and "direct
action" substituted. Oddly enough, Roller couples
with this a general strike in Belgium in 1893, which
met with some success, but it was political in its aim.
Nine years later, Belgian socialists rose again, but
leaders like Vandervelde and Anseele are blamed by
this writer because they call off the use of revolvers.
The strike of the Amsterdam dockers in 1903 is called
"a brilliant victory," because it began with such high
hopes. Its final "failure" was owing to "social parasites," a term he fixes upon socialists who "posted
proclamations which declared the strike off," and thus
prevented it "from spreading over the whole country
and becoming general and consequently was lost."
The truth is that a very reckless anarchist leadership
frightened the socialist party into a use of its strength
to save a situation that had become impossible. It
was necessary to reach the farm laborer, who proved
to be beyond the reach of the anarchist appeal,
though Mr. Roller tells us in the following words how

[1] Another general strike to which Syndicalists point is that which
silenced scores of industries in Australia and New Zealand in the
summer of 1890. Few strikes have been followed by consequences
so momentous. It was revolutionary in the strictest sense because it
shifted the political powers of the state. It has one advantage over
Russian, Spanish, and other obscure strikes which serve as syndicalist
patterns, because the facts are much more clearly before us.

they should have proceeded: "Nothing is as contagious and suggestive as rebellion. The farm workers and the poor farmers might imitate the workers of the cities and seize the possessions of great land owners. In recent years it has happened quite frequently that the striking workingmen marched out into the country, in the villages near the cities, enlightened the farmers and won them by saying to them: 'You don't need to pay any more taxes to the state, nor more rents to the landlord, nor more interest to the loan sharks, and to the owners of your mortgages—we just burn up all those papers.'"

These writers have not even told us a half truth on this subject. As exhibitions of discontent and organized protest, several of them have led to concessions, but their influence in this has been precisely that of any old-fashioned strike. The dramatic event of which so much has been written (the post office strike in France), compelled attention to undeniable grievances, but now that the facts of the "second strike" are known, it is a queer judgment that can see in them "great successes." [1]

[1] In a contribution just made to the *New York Call* is a wiser judgment. "Our friends of the I. W. W. have a great deal to say about the general strike. Now, I have seen one general strike in operation. That was in Holland in 1902, and I must say that it somewhat reminds me of the story of the man who was night after night disturbed by a dog howling in front of his house. One night, no longer being able to stand the racket, he ran out in his nightshirt, in spite of the fact that it was bitterly cold, to silence the dog. When he failed to return after an hour his wife went out to look for him. She found him lying full length upon the snow, stiff with the cold, holding on to the dog's tail. 'What in the world are you trying to do?' she asked him. And he answered in a weak voice: 'I am trying to freeze the dog to death.' (Laughter.) Now, when we try to starve the capi-

Apart from its political uses, the "general strike" has been found to be a weapon so dangerous to labor that no instance can be shown of its *economic* triumph. No one has seen this so clearly as the socialist leaders in every country. If Jaurès, Kautsky, Vandevelde flirt with it, they make it clear that its uses are political. Able studies like that by Henriette Roland-Holst,[1] are not lacking in radical exposition, but it is the political possibilities that are given weight. These leaders feared the very thing that has happened in Sweden, France, and England since the Swedish "general strike" in 1909—namely, *its increasing uncontrollable economic disorders.*[2] Never was a great strike conducted with less lawlessness than that in Stockholm: never one with more restraint on the part of the State. So careful were the strikers, that they kept their men at work at many points (as lighting and water works) where the public would too keenly suffer. The men coöperated with the police and against open saloon traffic. With more than a quarter of a million men on strike, the opportunity was never fairer for a real trial of this device. When from every source "the rich, the half-rich and their hangers-on" went heartily to work at every sort of job, the leaders said this was to be expected. But this "social uprising" against the strike spread rapidly be-

talists into submission they are very likely to beat us at the game. They are able to lay up provisions and to buy up what provisions there are on the market, while we are not." The writer expresses the hope that workingmen's coöperation may develop an economic strength on which labor may at last rely for its own support.

[1] See also *General-Streik und Sozialdemokratie*, Dresden, 1906.

[2] See also *Der Politische Massenstreik*, by Eduard Bernstein, Breslau, 1905.

yond the capitalist and bourgeois classes; it appeared
sullenly in the labor ranks.   Several thousand agricul-
turists had been organized, but they could not be kept
from furnishing food to the public, because they saw
the greater number of their neighbors (who were not
organized) making good money.   The man on the land
would not recognize his interests as one with city labor.

Even within the city, as the little shops stopped
credit and the promised funds from foreign trade
unions proved pitiably inadequate, a large labor contingent began to grumble.   Their families were already on the verge of suffering.

It is known that the industrial world generally lives
from hand to mouth; that all our available food supplies would vanish in a few weeks if production were
actually to stop.   Every trade union, no matter how
imposing a figure its funds have reached, sees these
accumulations disappear with shocking rapidity when
its main membership lays down its tools.   This lesson
came with gloomy surprise in the Swedish city.

Seven years before, a purely political strike against
gross irregularities in the suffrage had left a tradition
of hope in favor of the "general economic strike."
The analogy proved deceptive.   The "strike," moreover, became largely a lockout against claims set up
by the younger and more radical "socialist league."
Syndicalists may get this crumb of comfort from the
failure of this strike.   It seems to have produced a
considerable anti-trade union and anti-political movement, *because* it failed.   They now have their daily
paper and a fighting organization.

There is not a practical use to which one of these

syndicalist weapons can be put that does not raise the question of violence and its relation to the propaganda. In a publication just from the press [1] one reads (p. 26): " If the ruling class of today decide as its prototypes of the past have decided, that violence will be the arbiter of the question, then we will cheerfully accept their decision and meet them to the best of our ability and we do not fear the result." "The I. W. W.," it says, has now "come to the knowledge that justice, liberty, rights, &c. are but empty words, and power alone is real. Refusing to even try to delegate its power, it stands committed to the policy of direct action."

In the following chapter we shall see that its culmination is in the general strike which French anarchists define as identical with the social revolution. We shall see the theoretic justification of any unpleasantness which might follow direct action, namely, that "the property owners who own all of us," safe behind the mask of laws made in their own defense, practice *indirect* action to keep power from the people. Because of this exclusion labor, it is said, has no choice but in action that is "direct." The general strike thus becomes in Griffuehle's words, "the conscious explosion of labor's efforts to free itself." [2] In its last expression it is the taking possession of the world's machinery for the good of all—*au profit de tous*.

This *is* the revolution. Is violence to be expected? This, he says, depends wholly upon the attitude of the possessors. The general strike will be violent or pacific according to the amount of resistance to be overcome.

[1] *On the Firing Line*, P. O. Box 2129, Spokane, Wash.

[2] *L'Action Syndicaliste*, p. 32.

XI

"DIRECT ACTION"

NEITHER sabotage nor "direct action" is quite fairly explained apart from certain economic beliefs of those who now adopt them. The struggle of labor against capitalism is consciously directed by Syndicalism to gain control at the *centers and sources of economic power*. In the most popular literature attention is perpetually called to the "concentration of industrial forces" which is believed to change the whole method of warfare. There is no denial that the older trade unions were fighting intelligently with "contracts" and "agreements" but combination and the modern trust are said to have wrought a revolution which requires other means.

When Monsieur Pataud three years ago found himself at an electric center of such power in Paris, when he realized that he had only to "make a gesture" and the great city was at his mercy, he furnished one of many illustrations of what these new agencies may enable syndicalists to accomplish. "We have," he said, "to teach labor that the lever to lift the world is already in its hand." "Make labor conscious of its place and power and the battle is won." Behind this belief is much reasoned explanation meant to justify "direct action." Capitalism from the beginning has known and practiced every form of "indirect action" over labor. With the help of others in the upper classes, laws have been made to keep economic forces safely in their own keeping. But modern organization so shifts production from one plant to another as to defeat every real purpose of the trade union. By "contracts" of different dates, it can keep one union at work while another is on strike.

" If in a mine, the engineers and pumpmen remain faithful to such a contract, the owners can prevent the flooding of the mines and thus hold out until the other workers are starved back to the job."

All these immense resources of indirect action capital controls. It has besides the exact counterpart of every labor weapon—lockout, blacklist, its own agent or "walking delegate." If its profits are in danger, capitalism can "ca canny," and restrict the product on a scale to make bricklayers mad with envy. But chief of all is capital's stupendous power through law and politics of its own making. Through the delays and subterfuges of legislatures, through the labored technique of court decisions, the claims of the worker are held at bay.

All this is the "indirect action" of those who hold the keys of economic power. Against these shrewd indirections, Syndicalists will now pit their own direct strategy.

Slowly the dulled brain of labor has discovered its helplessness. It has been deceived by a succession of petty concessions in wages, hours and conditions, but the grim fact of its dependence and insecurity has at last grown clear. "Direct action" is labor's weapon against all the astute indirections of capital.

When Mr. Ettor and his friends were released at
Salem, he immediately told the thronging crowd met
to greet him, that they and such as they, were his real
deliverers. He had been rather complimentary to the
court and did not think ill of it, but for his freedom,
he thanked the enthusiasm and devotion of the
workers. These had sent money and lawyers but,
more than all, had roused a sustaining pressure of
public opinion that was irresistible. In Victor Griffuehle's exposition of syndicalist action is found the
same explanation of the freeing of Dreyfus.[1] "This
wronged man was not let off by the courts—they would
have killed him or banished him fast enough—but by
noisy volcanic agitation in the street, press, parlor—
even by scenes of rank violence," according to the trade
union secretary, this electric atmosphere was behind
the timid legalities, forcing them to take account of
it. In the light of this reasoning, Syndicalists now go
to their new tasks. If it is asked, why labor does not
also appeal to politics; why, with its overwhelming
numbers, it does not organize to elect its own representatives and thus create a new legal order in its
own favor, it has this answer: "We have been watching that fatuous game for a generation. Political
democracy and all 'reformist' socialism have tried
that so long and in so many parts of the world, that
we see its uselessness. The best fellows we send to
legislatures, to mayor's chairs, or to ministries, lose
their heads. Not one of them who breathes that atmosphere two years but comes back to us a changed
man. It is a crooked road that makes crooked men.

[1] *L'Action Syndicaliste*, p. 23.

We have found now a road that leads straight where we want to go."

This road is direct action.   With ironical by-play, the writers and speakers tell us that capitalism has been their one great teacher in the ways of direct action and of sabotage.   "We have many times used chemicals to spoil products, but the private profit-makers taught us everything we know, by making us partners in all the lying processes of adulteration. In trying to defraud the consumer, they have educated us.   We have had to connive and help in this whole cheating process,—clothing, candies, building materials, paints, spices, bread, soups, and a hundred others in commonest use—we have been instructed to the last detail, how to cheat the consumer into the belief that he was getting one thing, when he was getting what he never would have touched had he known the truth."   "Did the soldiers in Cuba eat Chicago 'embalmed beef' when they found it out?"

In one of the most recent I. W. W. pamphlets are the following passages meant for instruction.   They illustrate "direct action" assuming forms scarcely distinguished from sabotage.[1]

"A glance over the yearly reports of health and poor food commissions and government inspectors will reveal a few facts to the point.   Here we see that millions of eggs are condemned in the store houses.   The food commissioners discover that there are 'spots' No. 1 and spots No. 2 and 'Roses' in the market.   These spots and roses, sorted according to the degree that

[1] *Direct Action and Sabotage*, W. E. Trautmann, p. 23.

the rosening or rottening process has reached, are used mostly in bakeries for pies and cakes, and bread. The bakery worker knows it, is aware of it since ever bakeshop slaves had to work in dirty, filthy, vermin-invested workshops. His job is supposed to make him immune against the effects of perfumes and deteriorated flour. He has to mix it in so that everybody will believe and think that the bakeshops, small and large, are operated under the most sanitary conditions. So these millions of 'spots' are backed in and nicely mixed by the worker in the bakeshop. These cakes and pies are mostly sold to the poorer people, their stomach is hardened anyway by the adulterated stuff they consume every day without knowing it. The effects of this slow poisoning process are scarcely noticed."

"But what a howl would go up,—in fact, we heard quite often the furore that these statements of plain facts have created,—if the bakery workers on a nice day, all together, would announce that the 'spots' and 'roses' are all in abundant quantity baked into a certain assortment of baked wares. The consumer is warned of the possibilities,—who ever gets one of these 'rose embalmed' pies is himself only to blame if his stomach gets out of commission."

"Every candy maker knows that 'terra alba,' a white clay, is used in such proportions that it would shock the gumchewers if they knew how much of that indigestible stuff wanders into the stomachs of the fair ladies. Throwing in sugar and other ingredients the candyworker is supposed to let the machines work the mixing to perfection, the worker tends the machine, he is supposed to see nothing when that 'terra alba' is squeezed through the mixer.

"Are the workers supposed to be the capitalists' keepers and help protect them against the effects of their quiet, legitimate business affairs? Terra alba may get into a heap of candy stuff in big chunks, unmixed. The workers turn that instrument against their own oppressors.

"We have only to take a leaf from the employers' own book."

With corrosive irony one of our I. W. W. papers copies opinions from many of our most distinguished citizens on the lawlessness of our various "trusts" and large combinations. "Do we need," he asks, "any other pedagogues? Do they not show us day by day how to get what they want against the law or outside the law?" "The Government, great lawyers, and top-lofty politicians in both houses are all sweating together to keep these giants of industry within the law and *can't do it*."

"All these moral examples make our way easy." "According to their own account, their indirect action is as lawless as our direct action and not half so successful in the attempts to conceal it."

In the application of this principle, we are never certain whether sabotage or direct action is meant. Under the heading of sabotage, many of the illustrations are the exact counterpart of what others call "direct action." Yvetot's *A. B. C. du Syndicalisme* is filled with them. He defines "direct action" as any method which drives the employer (*à faire céder le patron*), either by interest or fear, to yield to labor's demand.

Because it is a war without truce, all "time contracts" are anathema. When a trade union journal twits the I. W. W. with entering into such agreements, the eastern organ, *Solidarity* admits that in a single instance this was done by a Montana local. When this "violation of the principle and practice of the I. W. W." was discovered, the local was punished by the withdrawal of its charter.

There is little significance in a war policy so extreme, unless our business system is believed to be so near its end that it can be disabled and overcome by guerilla tactics such as these.

When a leader like Tom Mann in England warns his followers against making any agreement except of the most temporary nature with the managers of capital; when he tells them that every provision for peace between the two parties is a perpetrated wrong on labor, we see the whole relation set squarely on a war footing, and its chosen weapons are those of war. Old-fashioned strikes are to go on, but with a new purpose. They are to be quick and sharp in order to save ammunition. The men, even when striking, are "to keep at work, but spoil the product." They are "suddenly to return to their jobs before strike-breakers appear, but to drop work again until the boss is tired out." The short strike is not only to pester the employer; it is, like army drill, to become the school of practice in preparation for the coming general or universal strike. French syndicalists actually use the word *grèviculture* (strike culture) as if strikes could be nursed and grown like plants in a garden.[1]

---

[1] Griffuehles in *L'Action Syndicaliste* uses another figure, that of the gymnasium in which all practice is like that of army manœuvers.

Behind all this is the assumption that the business man representing capitalism, can be worried into submission by losses in the shop and mill. This again takes for granted two things: first, the decrepitude of our business system and, secondly, the ability and preparedness of labor (as defined by Syndicalists) to take over and administer capitalist production. The saner among them do not claim that this can be done "at once," but only as capitalist management is worn out by the unremitting plague which labor can inflict on capital by refusing any longer to play the capitalist game. "From now on," says Tom Mann, "we know the enemy and how to deal with him."

It is flatly impossible to take with much seriousness either of these claims. With whatever brutalities and vices the present business system is infected; whatever the measure of its wrongs to labor, it is not yet in a state of decrepitude, neither are wage earners, without many decades of training, within sight of power or fitness to manage the main enginery of capitalism, finance, transportation, and the great industries.

It is among things conceivable that two or three generations of discipline, especially in productive co-operation, may give labor essential mastery over this enginery. But it must be said with a certainty that needs no revision, that this discipline and capacity will not be acquired through habits and modes of thought made by the practiced negations of strikes, boycotts, and sabotage.

As this volume goes to press, an Article on Direct Action appears in *The Independent*, Jan. 9th, by a writer for the French *La Bataille Syndicaliste.* It has the more value, as it was "passed upon" by Haywood, Bohn and Ettor—the two former associate editors on the *International Socialist Review.* The writer, Mr. André Tridon, shows at once how difficult it is to distinguish direct action from sabotage. Both alike are schools of solemn and vigorous instruction for the destruction of capitalism. Syndicalists, he assures us, "do not recognize the employer's right to live any more than a physican recognizes the right of typhoid bacilli to thrive at the expense of a patient, the patient merely keeping alive." He shows the importance of studying market conditions so that the blow may fall when the employer is "rushed with orders." Two syndicalist veterans, Pouget and Faure, have recently dealt with "technical instruction as revolution's handmaid" which Mr. Tridon offers us for up-to-date suggestiveness.

"The electrical industry is one of the most important industries, as an interruption in the current means a lack of light and power in factories; it also means a reduction in the means of transportation and a stoppage of the telegraph and telephone systems.

"How can the power be cut off? By curtailing in the mine the output of the coal necessary for feeding the machinery or stopping the coal cars on their way to the electrical plants. If the fuel reaches its destination what is simpler than to set the pockets on fire and have the coal burn in the yards instead of the furnaces? It is child's play to put out of work the elevators and other automatic devices which carry coal to the fireroom.

"To put boilers out of order use explosives or silicates or a plain glass bottle which thrown on the glowing coals hinders the combustion and clogs up the smoke exhausts. You can also use acids to corrode boiler tubes; acid fumes will ruin cylinders and piston rods. A small quantity of some corrosive substance, a handful of emery will be the end of oil cups. When it comes to dynamos or transformers, short circuits and inversions of poles can be easily managed. Underground cables can be destroyed by fire, water, plyers or explosives, etc., etc."

Here we see the "saving power of the revolution" transferred from the field of politics and reform to the nerve centers of production. Here the "system" is to be paralyzed by the daring of "small, energetic minorities" through direct action. Never a satisfying word is given us as to what these daring minorities are to do with the majorities after the system is smitten. How are the beaten majorities to be convinced and managed? In the familiar patois of the Anarchist, we are reminded that "minorities are always in the right." This is not Frederick Douglas, "One with God is a majority" but "A minority with God is a majority." [1]

[1] Pouget defines this minority privilege with great precision. It is to be vividly conscious of its purpose, because the dull masses of the majority have to be spurred and whipped into line. So dull is this majority that it must be treated as so many " nullities."

XII

SABOTAGE

As the meaning of the word gentleman depends upon the person who speaks it, sabotage is the most doubtful of terms until we know something of him who uses it. Like the term "direct action," if one is inclined to violence, sabotage readily lends itself to extreme measures. In the thick of a desperate and losing strike, it has many times meant outrageous ruin to property.

In the early stage of the discussion in Germany, a Syndicalist saw in his paper an account of some slight accident in the machinery of the Belfast Rope Works, whereby four thousand men were instantly left in idleness. This came to him like one of those happy accidents which has so often led to great scientific discoveries. Just a little break in the machinery and four thousand men must stop! A hint like that was not to be lost. If properly reasoned out, it might be "utilized for great social purposes." To elevate such accidents into a social policy; to instruct labor in the art of turning blind casualties into a planned on-slaught against capitalism is "a project to stir men's blood." After this manner the delighted discoverer reasoned about this thrilling invention. Like many another invention, the thing itself has far off origins.

From the wooden shoe of the peasant, *sabot*, it has acquired all its mischievous significance. A French syndicalist says it became popular after striking weavers, in 1834 in Lyons, had smashed both glass and machines with their heavy foot-gear.

A university professor of France has traced for me some further niceties in the history of the word, but for our main purpose it has no difficulties. In substance, it is as old as the strike itself. It is a specialized form of making trouble for the employer. Trade unions have been as familiar with its uses as with any other weapon in their fighting career. It is the familiar "ca canny" of the Scotch which got much advertising at the strike of Glasgow dockers in 1889. They had asked a rise of wages which was refused. The union official instructed the men in sabotage. Farm laborers had been brought in to fill the places of the strikers. "Let us go back to the job," said the official, "and do it exactly as the land lubbers do it. Those butter-fingers break things and drop things into the water from the docks. See to it, lads, that you imitate them until the masters learn their lesson." "If they like that kind of work, let them have plenty of it."

It is such as these in great numbers and from many countries that I. W. W. instructors give us for illustration. A father of Syndicalism, Emil Pouget, writes expressly on sabotage partly, it seems, to assure the outside public that (as consumer) it need have no fear. "Sabotage is solely against the boss."

In recent strikes among bakers, the bread in its early stages has been spoiled by some unappetizing addition, (like castor oil or petroleum) to the dough. Though it cannot be eaten, the eater is reassured by

M. Pouget that in no case is it poisoned,—unpalatable, yes; "but not injurious to health."

In California, during the strike on the Harriman roads, a machinist who had left his job made the same distinction. "We refuse," he said, "to put the public to serious risk. We can manipulate the machinery easy enough—from the engines to the track, we can put big trouble and big expense onto the managers." Another told me, "We'll bleed that crowd white before we get through. We've forced them to hire an army of spies and Pinkertons. They talk cheerful to the public, but we'll take so many millions out of them that they will think more than twice before turning us down again." He too, like M. Pouget, was sure that the public was safe, but his reasoning was even less reassuring.

The variety of these practices is as diverse as modern industry itself. In the life of that famous utopian, Fourier, we are told that his first moral revolt against the competitive system came to him when he discovered that as clerk he was expected to lie to the purchaser whenever necessary. Of great spiritual sensitiveness, he could not bring himself to this and went on blurting out the truth about the various wares until the infuriated employer turned him from the shop.

I have sometimes heard this delicate cruelty of exact truth telling recommended by the I. W. W. as one of the most perfected forms of sabotage for clerks and retail vendors generally. "Get together, study the foods, spices, candies, and every adulterated product. Study the weights and measures, and all of you tell the exact truth to every customer."

This is near akin to something far more widely practiced. For railway employees to submit an exact
obedience to every rule under which they work, is to
create instant havoc on that road. A train is not
started on schedule tick while two or three old ladies
are in the act of climbing onto the car. There has
always to be the "margin of discretion" in applying
rules. French and Italian Syndicalists brought utmost confusion to the railroads by their "conspiracy
of literal obedience." It is one of the French phrases,
"Study the time, the condition of trade, the technique
of the machinery. Wherever you find the most
sensitive nerve—attack it with *acute refinement.*" In
a French restaurant an objectionable employer was
driven half insane on finding that his waiters were
serving guests, as publicly advertised, "with perfectly fresh foods." They were practicing sabotage
by dropping out all the traditional ingenuities through
which half-spoiled material could be given artistic
satisfaction to the eater. The cutters in a tailors'
strike won their contest by preparing garments up to
the standard promised by the proprietor, but with a
finished excellence which left him with a deficit.

In Bordeaux gas works, scabs were kept from the
establishment by the strikers' following the contract
and remaining at their posts, but doing their work
so as to shower the managers with public complaint.

If the resources of sabotage are made a study; if all
its possibilities are investigated and the results turned
into suggestive material for general use, it may become
a rare and exciting sport. It is as easy on the farm as

on the railroad. These finer points of the game have thus far had little use in the United States. They only appear in literary form as hints for talents and occasions that may in time arise. That we may some time have a "university of the proletariat" for still wider instruction appears in a report published in Paris two years ago, in which definite instruction is given as to the various forms of sabotage and their uses in different industries. Both authors of this document are confessed Anarchists, one of them having resigned from the socialist section to which he had belonged. As long as machinery is owned by employers, says the report, "it is the enemy of the man who operates it. Its private possession must be made so vexatious and troublesome that no man will care to own it. 'Then labor will come by its own.' That sabotage can be carried on without money is thought to be one of its chief advantages. This propaganda is 'the great university of the proletariat.'"

The talents developed thus far by our I. W. W. have not shown themselves in "acute refinements." In northwestern saw mills timber lengths were changed so that only misfits were left for the planned structure. Logs were so laid that in sawing half the value was lost. Nails were so driven as to damage the saw and in the hauling from the woods, teams, harnesses and tools were "skilfully injured."

A group of our Italian excavators met a cut in their wages by straightway taking their shovels to a machine which clipped from the blade enough of its surface to correspond to the cut in wages. They sent in their explanation: "Less pay, less shovel." A good translation of *à mauvaise paie mauvais travail.*

The advantages which are supposed to follow a shrewd use of sabotage are that it enables the men to hold their job, even while half ruining it. The risk and waste of long strikes have been learned. Sabotage, "if made an intellectual process," may strike at the employer a swifter and more deadly blow and lessen the chances of scabbing.

In order to show the easy resources of sabotage, Emile Pouget rather vauntingly puts down a list of rare accomplishments during only twenty days of July, 1910, when telegraph and telephone lines were cut to the number of 795. Instruction is given to show what can be done with "only two cents' worth of chemicals to spoil machine products."

The *Technical World* reports an I. W. W. strike in British Columbia that shows the strategy among highly paid labor. In the official statement of the general secretary, it is laid down as a principle of action that only by the exercise of power can the slightest concession be won from capital.[1] During strikes, he says:

"The works are closely picketed and every effort made to keep the employers from getting workers into the shops. All supplies are cut off from strike bound shops. All shipments are refused or missent, delayed and lost if possible. Strike breakers are also isolated to the full extent of the power of the organization. Interference by the government is resented by open violation of the government's orders, going to jail *en*

[1] *I. W. W. History,* p. 17.

masse, causing expense to the taxpayers—which are but another name for the employing class.

"In short, the I. W. W. advocates the use of militant 'direct action' tactics to the full extent of our power to make good."

The above extract rewards study. It is not a product of soap-box oratory. It is coolly written down in the official history. Government "interference" is to be met by "open violation." The general body of taxpayers is identified with the employing class, thus turning into an enemy of labor, all those who support the government by paying taxes. Against these, militant direct action is to be used upon the one principle, the degree of strategic power possessed by strikers.

Such peculiarity as there is in syndicalist teaching on this point is to make it an object of instruction, to make it more universal, more conscious and more ingeniously adapted to its end.

A foreman in a textile mill told me the racy details of sabotage as practiced in his own department. Its cunning effectiveness was such, in his opinion, that only concerted action and a good deal of tutoring by the more clever men could account for the result. The I. W. W. journals have an ample stock of informing suggestions to show the high values of this invention. A little half-heartedly they insist that violence is stupid, because the objects of sabotage can be reached with more subtle effectiveness without it. "If a teamster scabs,—don't hit him, but just hide the axle nuts of his wagon and put some artistic cuts in his harnesses." Much is said of sabotage as "a labor-saving device." "We make the machinery of production go on strike, instead of ourselves. If we strike too, that is incidental."

In one of the severer struggles in western Canada an I. W. W. reporter states the wages of the teamsters at three dollars a day with board, and the common shoveler at two seventy-five. These men disliked piece work and the required purchase of dynamite from the boss. As it was "contrary to principles," more than 700 of them "go out at the drop of the hat," without making any demands whatever. Their relations once severed, they act in the spirit of Syndicalists trained for their task. Then came formal presentation of grievances; here and there, shorter working time, changes in the contract system, and better fare at table. Word went out that no violence would be permitted by the strikers; they even organized their own police. They took severe measures against the too free sale of liquor in the saloons— "only one drink a day." The strike-breakers hurried on from the coast were met and persuaded to return. I. W. W. men put in jail for "unlawful assembly" were paid by the strikers one dollar daily "for the common good." "Let a few hundred of us go to jail," it was said, "and see if the province likes the expense." The forms of sabotage were discussed. It was easy to have "accidental fall of rocks or embankments." If strike-breakers got through, they were to be hospitably met with hot coffee. "There may be something in that coffee—a pause—sugar of course." The striker chosen to instruct the reporter says, "Before they get through, they will find it cheaper to make terms with

us than fight us. 'I Won't Works' they call us. They
are right. 'I Won't Works' *for capital*."

He then continues: "We are striking to educate the
workers to their power—to show them if they unite that
they can paralyze every wheel of industry and compel
the expropriation of all industry from that side of the
line to this side of the line; from capital to labor. That
is where our organization differs from all other organizations. You think we are beaten? We will go back to
work and accumulate funds; and strike yet again,
till the public finds it cheaper for us to operate all
industry than to tolerate the recurring deadlock. We
are striking solely to overthrow the capital system.
First, in England, it was the railways. Then, it was
the coal mines. Now, it is the docks. Here we have
begun operations because labor is so scarce that we
can show our power. We have tied up one road for
two months. Next time, we'll tie up three roads for
three months; and so we'll go on and educate and
educate and educate labor to a knowledge of its own
strength and solidarity till it realizes it has only to
unite in order to take over all industry and overthrow
the capital system."

That Canada has for this very kind of disagreement,
the best of all Arbitration Acts, was well known to the
men. They even discussed it, but no appeal to it was
allowed, as the strikers were "not out to patch
things up." "We are out against the wage system
itself."

The truth about sabotage is that its essence is destruction. All the dulcet phrases about "mere passive
resistance," "only fold the arms or put your hands

in your pockets and keep them there," or, as I heard a speaker say, "Why, you've nothing to do but just stand round and look sweet,"—all this does not hide the fact that the machinery of production is stopped and to that extent product (wealth) is destroyed. "Quietly change the address on freight cars filled with perishable foods, so they shall go one or two hundred miles south instead of north to Paris, and then get side-tracked a few days more," was one among many guiding hints to the railway strikers. It sounds as gentle as a friendly salute or as the pretty French name, *la grève perlée*,[1] for a strike that may be ugly in the extreme.

With time, the sabotier has, like the rest of us, gained civility and intelligence. He does not burn and wreck every new machine in sight like his English brothers seventy years ago, or Russian peasants a generation later. But his gain in humor and affability does not imply that he is one whit less a destroyer that his ruthless forerunner.

We have not forgotten the advice of the " Grand Master " of the Knights of Labor, that every work-man after drinking smash his beer bottle. How much work it would give to labor! How many unemployed could at once be set to work!

Yes, but why stop at beer bottles ? Why not also break milk bottles, tea cups, plates and then, when the meal is finished, break up the table and chairs,

---

[1] Of this term la grève perlée, Professor Ernest Dimnet writes me, "It is railway slang. For several months the men just changed the addresses stuck on the cars, so they (the cars) were as hard to find as pearls that had dropped off the string."

destroy the carpet, and finally the house ?—One and all—it would "make work."

On the same witless level is this whole annihilating scheme, recommended and urged upon crowds and individuals whose action is beyond control.

Fortunately, a large part of the labor world has learned that the mere smashing of machines is only heady stupidity. The labor of the future will learn that sabotage *set up as a principle*, or loosely advised, is an economic silliness because it is destructive. It means a deliberated lessening of products—a process in its aftermath always deadlier to the weak than to the strong. It has a grim pathos to hear the strongest man in our I. W. W. crusade congratulating a great and enraptured audience upon the successes of the latest English strike. It was bungled from the start and marked by horrors of suffering that made strong men sick to look upon.

No strike ever "succeeded" that was not encouraged and directed by some measure of practical wisdom. A strike, like any other rude force, is so much power applied for a specific object. It does not "succeed" because it is a strike. If it succeeds, it is only by virtue of shrewd and skilful adaptation to time, to place, and to conditions.

In many ways sabotage has more hazards—more risks of failure—because it is secret, underhand, and so easily beyond all control by those who recommend it. We are told it is "so easy," "so noiseless," "so sheltered." Yes, and so is an administered poison easy, noiseless, sheltered, but it is not necessarily good sense to recommend its indiscriminate use.

Sabotage is not unlike a poison shot into an organism, but it is an organism of which every laboring man and woman is vitally a part. It is a poison that will never reach capital as something wholly separate from labor. The many who are nearest to the margin of want will suffer, first and in the end, most poignantly.

Very perfectly the wiser men in the socialist movement have learned this lesson. It may have lacked practical tact, that a few months ago, the socialist officials should vote expulsion from the party of all those who preached sabotage. This may have made "a too irritating issue" at the moment. But the kind of miscellaneous advocacy given to sabotage in this country deserves all that was meant by that action. Through its trade unions and through socialistic organization, labor has got at last quite organic strength enough to choose and hold fast to constructive plans. Every hour devoted to destruction is a weakening of its cause. This criticism refers solely to sabotage as actually taught and commended. So long as the fact of warfare in our industrial system continues, the strike, boycott, and sabotage will have a place in spite of the waste and disorder that follows. All of us together must endure them, as war is suffered, until we learn the sanity and moral self-restraint to substitute enlightened and constructive measures in our human intercourse.

The incurable vice of sabotage is in the kind of general doctrinal emphasis given it. Its logic is that of the class-war elevated into a principle and recommended to excited crowds. Its practical dangers are in the immediate consequences which the heated imagination is sure to draw from such advice.

It is not alone Socialists of penetration and maturity who see this, but Syndicalists themselves lift a warning finger. Lagardelle is now reported by Kautsky to be dismayed at the *exhaustion* which this destructive passion has brought with it. The possibilities of the strike and sabotage (as one weapon in its armory) are as sacred to him as ever, but he sees the havoc of any general popularizing of such a force. This vigorous propagandist of syndicalism said in 1907:

"If socialism consists wholly of the class struggle, socialism is as a matter of fact entirely contained within syndicalism, for outside of syndicalism there is no class struggle."

He objects to the Anarchists because they make too light of the class struggle or are merely muddle-headed about it. It is to him the greatness of Syndicalism that it has shown the proletariat to be the only section of society to which we may look for salvation. Nothing is to be hoped from political democracy, because it is engaged in the ignoble trickery of binding the classes closer together. The break, he says, must be absolute. Then and then only can we hope that "*not one thing traditionally esteemed will survive destruction.*"

The disastrous folly of a teaching like this is the more amazing when we recall what it is that Syndicalism sets before us. It is "to capture the machinery of production." From the inside, where the millions are toiling, they are to "take possession" of transportation, mines, and factories; but they are to do this, as almost every leader says, by *showing themselves competent for the task*. They must "prove" their possession of skilled capacities equal to the great undertaking. This raises the question—is it then possible that a long and wide practice in destroying things is a part of such education? If sabotage is to go on among the masses until they "take over" the great machinery, what *habits* meantime will sabotage develop? Can they practice it for some decades as a fitting preparation for administrative tasks as stupendous as they are delicate? The question requires no answer. To give sabotage the prominence found in I. W. W. opinion is only a little less intelligent than was the attempt of European Anarchists, a few years before the appearance of Syndicalism, to beat the capitalist system by a large scheme of creating and circulating counterfeit money which began at once to circulate among the poorest and stupidest people. If capitalism is to be overthrown, it is not by crippling negations and mere mischief making. If it is to be conquered, it must be mainly by the slow creation of substitutes that have higher business efficiency.

The issues raised by sabotage have furnished continuous occasion for the sharpest differences in opinion, not only among Socialists but within the ranks of Syndicalism.[1]

---

[1] Already the organs of the I. W. W. are at swords' points with the acknowledged leaders of Socialism in the United States. Any reader curious to follow this inner feud has only to subscribe for six months to a paper like the *Nationalist Socialist* and to *Solidarity*, the I. W. W.

The fine technically trained intelligence of Sorel showed a wholesome fear of sabotage and cried out lustily against it, as does also Edouard Berth. H. G. Wells is the easy peer of M. Sorel. He has M. Sorel's dislike for Fabian politics, but these features of Syndicalism offer him no possible plan of social development. It is to him merely "a spirit of conflict." It is "the cheap labor panacea to which the more passionate and less intelligent portion of the younger workers drift." It is the "tawdrification of the trade unionism" and even its dream is "an impossible social *fragmentation*." Kautsky and the uncompromising Guèsde who despises parliamentary action, are little less severe. I do not bring against the I. W. W. the hostile opinions of the Webbs, Keir Hardy, MacDonald and German leaders. Such opposition is to be expected. It is more serious when men as untrammeled as Sorel, Guèsde, Bax and Wells rise up against it. These writers, one and all, look upon sabotage as a clumsily out-of-date and reactionary device.

sheet in Newcastle, Pa. Even Mr. Debs is attacked for raising doubts about sabotage. Last week I cut from an I. W. W. paper the following:

"Sabotage repels the American worker," says Debs. That is not true. The American worker has used the methods of the sabotier right along. I witnessed as slick a piece of sabotage last week as was ever pulled off. Done right under the boss's eyes when he endeavored to speed the machines up. He did not recognize it as such, but he lowered the speed. Indifferent work is a form of sabotage. The American worker inclines to it when disposed to resent his treatment.

"The checker in freight houses, to my knowledge, often puts a package in the wrong car to avenge a fancied wrong. This is sabotage. I have seen in mining camps soap put in the blacksmith's tub to prevent a good temper being secured on the steel."

With still more severity W. J. Ghent says in the
Socialist National Organ: "To preach violence and
sabotage to the working class is to preach not a
working-class morality, not a socialist morality, but
a slave morality. It is the morality of Roman slaves
in the days of the empire. By lying, deceit, craft,
and theft they sought to lessen the evils of their lot.
They did not heroically strive for emancipation. They
acquiesced in and compromised with slavery, and
sought in cowardly ways only to mitigate its evils.
They did not, in any general sense, mend their lot.
The shrewd and adroit slave sometimes lightened his
own burdens, and sometimes the burdens of a small
group. But the slave system as a whole was not
affected by this form of resistance—if it may be called
by that term. Nor will the tenure of the capitalist
system be affected by a like policy." [1]

There are finally collective forms of sabotage very
popular against public and legal authorities. The
last one of many (Oct. 1, 1912) comes from the general
secretary of the I. W. W., calling for help to aid the

---

[1] Mr. Robert Hunter has just quoted Professor Herve (*Call*,
Jan. 10,) as the "most daring and brilliant of all advocates of direct
action and sabotage." This Syndicalist wrote of the recent German
Socialist Victory as follows: "We have, by means of our internal dissensions, our sterile discussions of personalities, developed a party
on the one hand and a general federation of labor on the other, equally
stagnant, with equally ridiculous inefficiency, treasuries without
money, journals without readers, and have engendered demoraliza-
tion, skepticism and disgust.

"In truth, I begin to ask myself if with our great phrases of insurrection, direct action, sabotage, and 'chasing the foxes,' we are not,
after all, from a revolutionary point of view, but little children beside
the Socialist voters of Germany."

suffering strikers in Little Falls, N. Y. The local jail is already well-filled, but this leading official of the order asks that it be straightway so choked that another prison must be built. He does not ask his own membership for anything so commonplace as money, but urges all who can, to journey thither for the sake of being jailed. As they said in Fresno, California, "The town won't mind a dozen or two in jail, but if they have to provide for several hundred of us, they'll get sick." Mr. St. John wants to make town authorities in Little Falls sick by overloading and tiring out every protective and legal agency.

This is the round-about method by sabotage of discouraging and discrediting our present social mechanism. It is evenly on par with putting castor oil in bread, sifting sand into delicate machinery, or laming the horses of scab teamsters by setting the shoe on the hoof so that the nail reaches the soft part of the foot.

Precisely this is what the general secretary asks for the still more delicate machinery of society. It is to be clogged and rendered useless. A mill foreman told me he found the I. W. W. in one of his rooms using the knee against the parts of a machine which he said was "delicate as a baby." "It ruined the product for an entire day because the damage could not be seen till the next morning." "It was so easily done," he said, "that I never could prove to others that any one man did it." "Any one of them could spoil thirty dollars' worth of product in two seconds," was his estimate.

This direct annihilation of property was not more thorough than filling jails in twenty different towns

and cities. I tried once to reckon up the cost of one
of these escapades in which nearly 200 men must have
lost more than 100,000 days' earnings.   There was
not a baker's dozen of them who could not have
had work in that community, if they had been willing
to do it.   They took long journeys in freight cars.
Some paid their fares. I saw others driven from their
hold beneath fast trains, and others I saw dropping
off, smeared with dirt, as we slowed into the next
station. The incidental public expenditure—lawyers,
police, court trials and jails—furnish ugly hints of this
colossal waste of values, actual and potential.   To
multiply this special instance by at least thirty, would
give us approximate estimates of the last year's destruction.

I am in this not laying blame alone upon I. W. W.
adventurers.   Many and deeper causes are behind
these adolescent pranks.   But this method of sabotage, as practiced by wandering crowds in conflict with
local police, is like its other forms of waste.   It is
purely destructive, as warfare and disease are destructive.

Explicitly the I. W. W. mean it for this purpose.
Capitalism, they tell us, can be reached in no
other way.   One who was conspicuous at Lawrence
told me, "Why, the only fright we gave the capitalists was by showing them that we had power to
bring their business and their profits to a dead standstill.   We taught them this, and at the same time gave
an object-lesson to our own side.   We had only to
point to the empty mills and say,—'Look at your
work. You see how helpless they are without you.

They can't weave a yard or make a dollar without you.'" That was a fact, just as a deficit, an accident, or death is a fact; but it is not a fact to rejoice in.

If the wage earners are to get possession of the mills, as is the dream of the I. W. W., by no conceivable means will they get them, except by decades of positive and coöperative work with those who now own and direct the invested capital which these mills represent. Never will they get them by the waste, the negations, and evil habits which sabotage begets. Preached generally and as a doctrine, it separates them from their object and weakens them in every capacity to attain it.

XIII

VIOLENCE

AMONG some of the ablest expositors of I. W. W. principles, there seems to me very little pretence that violence may not be necessary at certain stages and under certain conditions. They are now but just started on their journey. From political Socialism and craft unions they have cut loose. The ordinary strike best illustrates "direct action." [1] It begins locally in a mine or mill. It then reaches a higher form in "mass action" (the mass strike), which includes the industry. If those working over a whole industrial area go out together, we have the general strike. The "universal strike" arrives when so many workers go out in any country as to disable the main sources of production. At any point along the route, the "irritation strike," quick and mysterious in action, is a sort of gymnastic exercise to train and educate our coming masters. These irritants meantime are admirably calculated to unnerve the employer and prepare him the sooner for his exit.

From first to last this issue between the I. W. W. and existing society is a trial of main strength, an encounter in which moral concepts, as commonly un-

[1] The strike illustrates but does not accurately enough define "direct action" which assumes an unremitting and truceless war on capitalism. The old-fashioned strike with accessories of arbitration, "agreements" recognize the wage system. That recognition is unforgivable to direct actionists.

derstood, are rigidly and expressly excluded. Anything which protects the present order is for that reason "wrong." Acts which lead to its undoing are therefore "right." They have a most winning candor in stating their case. Rarely is there any taint of the purposed obscurity over alarming proposals which one sometimes finds among more sophisticated Socialists. Mr. Ettor, who is on the Executive Board of the I. W. W., puts it first in general terms but jovially and without concealment: We also hear it said that our efforts are dangerous. Yes, gentle reader, our ideas, our principles and object are certainly dangerous and menacing, applied by a united working class would shake society and certainly those who are now on top sumptuously feeding upon the good things they have not produced would feel the shock. To talk of peace between capital and labor is "stupid or knavish."

It is as if a Christian asked for peace with sin. Judges, attorneys, preachers and politicians are one and all the paid lackeys of capitalism:—the "kept-crew" hiding "under the silk skirts of Mesdames 'Law and Order,'"—"as desperate and brutal a crew as ever scuttled a ship or quartered a man." With this new classification of sinners, the way is plain. Under these shifting, fugitive terms "right and wrong," the appeal must be to power, "cold, unsentimental power." In further words of Mr. Ettor from the standpoint of accepted law, morals, religion, etc., the capitalists are considered right and justified in their control and ownership of industries and exploitation of labor because they have the means to hire, and have organized a gang that skulks under the name of "Law, Order and

Authority," that is well paid and well kept to interpret and execute laws in favor of the paymasters of course. The new ethical propaganda thus becomes clear. New conceptions of right and wrong must generate and permeate the workers. We must look on conduct and actions that advance the social and economic position of the working class as right, ethically, legally, religiously, socially and by every other measurement. That conduct and those actions which aid, help to maintain and give comfort to the capitalist class, we must consider as wrong by every standard. If definite contracts with employers have been freely entered into, labor has no obligation to keep them. Mr. Trautmann's words are: (Industrial Union Methods.)

"The industrial unionist, however, holds that there can be no agreement with the employers of labor, which the workers have to consider sacred and inviolable.

"Industrial unionists will therefore sign any pledge, and renounce even their organization, at times when they are not well prepared to give battle, or when market conditions render it advisable to lay low; but they will do just the reverse of what they had to agree to under duress, when occasion arises to gain advantages to the worker." To disobey court injunctions is a "duty."

The general secretary, Mr. St. John, writes in his I. W. W. History: "As a revolutionary organization the Industrial Workers of the World aims to use any and all tactics that will get the results sought with the least expenditure of time and energy. The tactics used are determined solely by the power of the organization to make good in their use. The question of 'right' and 'wrong' does not concern us." This removes all obscurity as to methods and their justification. Capital now has the power. It is the task of labor to get that power for itself. It is to take it from capitalists by direct action, sabotage, boycott, and the cumulative strike. The I. W. W. organs are now having rare sport over "trade union contortions" to explain the conviction and jailing of so many of its members.

Editorially *Solidarity* [1] thus comments:

"Doubtless all the owls of capitalism and 'political socialism,' (and especially the latter,) will labor and bring forth tedious dissertations on the 'folly of violence in conflicts between capital and labor.' We opine, however, that the I. W. W. will decline to join in this unholy medley of condemnation. Assuming that these men were really guilty of the 'jobs' charged against them, we may question the expediency of their methods, but we cannot question the sincerity of men who will stake their lives and liberty in behalf of their union. Indeed, we can only view the actions of these men as another incident in the class struggle—not perhaps as that struggle appears to fifth-story editors, lawyers and other saviours of the working class; but as it is viewed by the sturdy men who risk their lives daily that gigantic structures necessary to civilization may be put in place."

To those who fear only that the cause of labor may come into disrepute because of dynamite methods, the editor continues:

[1] Jan. 4, 1912.

"Nonsense! One year of capitalist violence will outweigh a thousand years of labor's 'peaceful' history. Must we meekly apologize for those of our kind who occasionally strike back under great provocation? The capitalist sowed the wind and reaped a little zephyr of a cyclone in this case under consideration. Let the blood be upon the heads of our masters!"

One of the editors of the *International Socialist Review*, Mr. Frank Bohn, writes (in the *Call*, Jan. 6th) on the thirty-three "Dynamiters" just imprisoned at Leavenworth. Like the McNamaras their colleagues, they are "the John Browns of the social revolution," they are "the soldiers of the working class." Today, he says, they are passing through the doors of the Leavenworth Prison. "Let every revolutionary worker in the land stand with bowed head as they pass. They are fighters of the working class. That is enough for us now."

"May every one of you thirty-three live to come out of the jail so that we may grasp you by the hand and welcome you as comrades into the ranks of an army which can never know defeat."

There seems but one intelligent inference to be drawn from these opinions. In no case in this volume have they been "torn from their context." I have excluded far more violent opinions than any which are quoted because, like sparks from a flint, they were struck out in the heat of excitement or had a wholly irresponsible origin. From the coolest statement of aim, of purpose and of method, intimidating and destructive action is as unavoidable as in any other form of warfare.[1]

I asked a writer in this propaganda what he meant by telling the public that violence was entirely excluded in their principles. He said that it was both unnecessary and unintelligent. "When we have the power," he added, "we have only to stand off. We need not take our hands out of our pockets or utter a threat." This worthy sentiment might be true if capitalism were really at the end of its tether; if labor were ready to assume its functions and had reached that degree of mastery essential to its control of the world's business. If we imagine this *end* to be attained, violence would be, in his words, "unnecessary and unintelligent." The trifling obstacle here is that none of these things have yet happened. It will be marvel enough if they happen in several generations.

Our solicitude about violence does not concern the far end of achieved power, when the conquerors could afford to "fold their arms," our concern is with the long intervening spaces between the now and the then. Can labor use its approved weapons—the five-fold strike, its ingenuities of sabotage—in the long tug before it brings capitalism to its knees, without violence? There is not a page in the history of our I. W. W., or of Syndicalism generally, to give this hope the slightest warrant and most Syndicalists are perfectly aware of the fact. The main battle is all before them, and both their weapons and their primary doctrine of the

---

[1] In the article quoted from *The Independent*, Mr. Tridon says, in this fight Syndicalists do not even pretend to observe the rules of civilized warfare. The flag of truce does not protect emissaries.

"class warfare" makes this issue of probable violence hardly worth discussion.[1]

It is a damaging objection to any body of principles which carries with it as practical necessities so much approved destruction as "direct action" and sabotage imply. Economic and cultural benefits which the race has thus far garnered are not to be dealt with after the jaunty manner of the I. W. W. It may have the frankest admission, that these social accumulations have grown up through every imperfection known to human cunning. Private appropriation has assumed excesses of inequality that now threaten us as insidiously as any other disease. We have learned that a large part of this inequality is artificial and unnecessary. There is no higher statesmanship in the world than that which now sees this, admits it, and aims constructively to correct it. But the crude simplicity of methods which assume violence is childishly incompetent for the task put upon it. No section of society would suffer from it as the weak would suffer. Whatever place Syndicalism makes for itself in the coöperative service of reform, its ways must be supplemented and controlled by those to whom experience has brought some enlightened sense of what society is and what so-

[1] In the *New Review*, Jan. 18, Mr. English Walling says: " Violence also is usually condoned on the unconsciously humorous ground that if the police and militia were not present, there would be little violence. No unions *advocate* violence, but none surrender to the law those among their members who succumb to temptation under critical or exceptional circumstances, and it is rarely that they do not furnish defense funds. Even the I. W. W. does not advocate violence, but it is more frank in its attitude towards it than the older unions.''

cial life is as expressed in industry. These have heights, depths, and complications of which the objects of our study have at least as much to learn as others.

I was told of a Pennsylvania farmer with keen intellectual interests who was led to study the I. W. W. propaganda. Having read a good deal about Socialism, he became so absorbed in this new and bolder variation, as to go a long distance to hear a lecturer. In the questions which followed, the speaker had said of a steel mill near Pittsburg, "We shall take it if we can get it. Everything in it that labor didn't make was stolen out of labor. We can't get it 'politically.' We shall take it directly just as soon as we have the power to do it. The capitalists have stolen from us since the mill was started, and we don't propose to pay 'em just because they've been robbing us."

The farmer was not satisfied with this easy account of things. Among other questions, he insisted upon knowing by what right the special set of laborers, who happened just then to be in the mill, proposed to take to themselves all that others before them had earned. "You who are now there didn't make the mill nor very much of the machinery. I've got a big well-stocked farm, but I made only part of it. My grandfather and his boys, my father and my brothers—all of us helped get it where it now is. Shall the hired men that I have now, come in and take it?" This farm had expensive machinery and was worked under the wage system as "capitalistically" as the mill, and the question was perfectly fair. Its greater simplicity brings out the fantastic impossibilities of remedying our industrial wrongs by any such rough and ready methods.

If "power" represented by the I. W. W. is to be used, as they warn us, "to any extent necessary to its purpose" and if capitalism still possesses a fraction of the strength which these adventurers ascribe to it, nothing short of violence in some form can deprive it of its possessions. Legal and political reforms and all the resources of taxation are excluded. To subdue capitalism by the strike, direct action and sabotage can have no meaning apart from the strategic uses which violence and intimidation offer.

Among the reasons why these vigors will fail, is that a most powerful section of the working classes will oppose them to a man. So obvious a fact seems not yet to have the least recognition.

It is true that among prosperous folk, there is much specious canting about the stupendous treasures which labor has stored in savings banks and such like institutions, but the cant of those who insist that labor has nothing, or nothing worth speaking about, is quite as offensive in its distortion.

The truth is that the accumulated savings of very humble people have helped to build every shop and mill and railroad in the land. Hundreds of millions of savings bank deposits and insurance funds are invested in the "machinery of production." It is a small part compared to ownership by the richer classes, but the man with a hundred dollars in the bank is as tenacious of his small savings as the rich are of their greater savings. Our revolutionists think this argument funny and preposterous, but it stands for a fact with which they will have to reckon in every first and last attempt "to take over" the productive and distributive machinery of this country.

All the fertile and stagey analogies of the French Revolution; the unwearying assertion that "capital has everything and labor nothing," are so grossly misleading that we can await results with perfect confidence. Small as they are, wage earners' savings in this country are altogether sufficient to create *multitudinous centers of resistance* against any paralyzing onslaught against these producing properties.

In a garment workers' strike in New York City, I stood on the street with the man who led it. Hundreds of Jews were pouring out of a public building in which the strike was under discussion. My companion pointed to them and said, "You would not think it, but there are not ten men in that crowd who haven't money in the bank. It isn't much, but it is enough to make every one of them a sort of conservative." I am not making the inane suggestion that these people have enough, or that the whole bulk of wage earners' savings in the land justifies a single iniquity in our system. Our present economic distribution is criminally unfair because so much of it is unnecessary and avoidable.

These evils, however, are not to be met by the popular I. W. W. methods. Some millions of wage earners and farmers have just enough interest in ways that are wiser and fairer to take good care of themselves against noisy minorities that have learned so little about the business world and of the ways through which it is to be reformed.

XIV

ANARCHISM

SYNDICALISM has much in common with Socialism but the very intensity of its emphasis carries it beyond what is organic in the socialist movement. The student is never sure in whose presence he stands—that of the Anarchist or that of the Socialist.

Syndicalism now comes with a new dialect.[1] There is much mocking of "reason" and much deification of impulse and feeling. There are the familiar warnings against the "law" and institutions. If these are rigid, violence may offer the only road to "freedom." We are put on our guard against too much reflection. This may lead to submission which is the slave's vice. So easy is it to reason ourselves into smooth acquiescence with ruling economic and social powers—ambition, desire of wealth, all that may place us among the flesh-pots and separate us from the human mass, that the Devil gets easy possession of our souls. But "feeling, nobly kindled into enthusiasm saves us from these servilities." Thus the new morality is to be free from all "calculating reflection." Think of a "calculating soldier." Think of his reflecting about his pay in front of the enemy! No, it is spontaneity

[1] This dialect is strikingly like much in that powerful anarchist book Stirners' *Der Einzige und sein Eigenthum*, especially in that part of the volume dealing with the "power" of the individual.

and enthusiasm he needs. What of the artist who dulls his vision by haggling and reckoning over his pay, or the inventor sinking his fine imagination in calculations over royalties! In figures like these syndicalist metaphysic deals. Thus Sorel dramatizes his "sublime myth" of the general strike. It calls like "unseen music in the night" to the deeper and more unselfish passions of the soul. Its power is that it cannot be proved. Only what is beyond proof moves us greatly. He despises sociology with its goggled pretence of laws and classified data on which reasoned prediction can be based. Far better is a philosophy half articulate with its cavernous depths, its terrors, its silences and its mysteries.[1] "The unspoiled soul of the proletariat" is to be initiated into these veiled places where "tired and sleeping masses of men" may be roused to a sense of their power. Only through disturbing and dramatic figures speaking to the imagination can they be made to look and listen.

Above all, in this awakening is the proletariat to learn that it is to have no mastery but its own. Such salvation as it wins must be solely through its own initiative and direction. When it says, "No God, no master," there are no reservations. Though Sorel makes much of religion as myth, the Syndicalists generally are not timid and discreet like so many Socialists on the subject of instituted religion. They turn against it because of what it asks. Christian virtues, like reverence, humility and obedience, are all

[1] Even from a scholar showing much sympathy with Professor Bergson—I have heard the phrase, "He is the Philosopher of the Unutterable."

"slave morals" and virile youth should be taught to despise them.

It is because the State stands for organized external force, using for its own ends armies, laws, courts, education, churches, flags, that it too becomes, as it does with the Anarchist, the arch enemy.

Sorel not only strikes at capitalism and at politics that is its handmaid, he strikes also at the high priest of scientific Socialism, Karl Marx. Sorel sees in Marx a fatalistic optimism about the future of capitalism with its industrial units growing ever bigger because they cannot help it. An inexorable evolution is crowding the victors into more compact bodies, until by very over-weight they fall like ripened fruit into collectivist possession. This is all too easy for Monsieur Sorel and he will have none of it. Marxism is already in a state of "decomposition," and to this effect he writes his little book.[1]

Not so blithely do things go just where we want them in this world. They move toward these desired ends, not of their own impelling, but only as we urge and direct them by our own will and creative energies. Thus the Philosopher Bergson appears upon the scene:—he of the "world that we ourselves create," with *la volenté créatrice.*

Rousseau is again revived. The real tyrant is the majority rule. To submit even for a year to an elected person is to submit *for that year* to tyranny, therefore, we will none of it. It is Walt Whitman's "never ending audacity of elected persons." It is Thoreau jailed in Concord for non-payment of taxes. It is Tolstoi with

[1] *La Decomposition du Marxism.*

his serene and enduring hatred of the State. The same anarchist protest is in the syndicalist Edouard Berth. He calls the State the supreme parasite—*le parasite par excellence*. It is the "great unproducer," like a vampire sucking the life blood of the nation.[1] Its armies, navies, police, courts, prisons, are logical forms of this concentration of power in the State. By the same reasoning parliaments and politics are enemies, and even democracy with its universal suffrage comes in for fiery criticism at the hands of many of these pungent expositors. An authoritative Syndicalist like Lagardelle holds that "The duel is on between democracy and a genuine working-class socialism." With hostility to the state, "patriotism" becomes a disease. Everywhere workmen must be taught to "think away" every frontier line that separates the nations. Only thus can the "cosmic brotherhood of man" round itself into completeness. Morality will take no higher flight than in contributing "the soldier's penny" to teach him infidelity to his superiors—to teach him just why and how capitalism is using him and fooling him to do its own dirty work.

In its theoretic statement, this is the "higher anarchy."

To associate the I. W. W. with a ruffian clutching a smoking bomb, is a silliness that need not detain us. It is true that no revolutionary movement is without its criminals. They were ubiquitous in our War of the Revolution. They followed the wake of Garibaldi, and Mazzini was never free from them. They were among the English Chartists, and never

[1] Edouard Berth: *Les Nouveaux Aspects du Socialisme.*

have been absent from Ireland's long struggle for self-rule. The I. W. W. will not escape this common destiny. It will attract to itself many extremely frail human creatures, but the movement as a whole is not to be condemned by these adherents or by the shabby device of using panicky terms like anarchist. To say that Syndicalism has strong anarchist tendencies is nevertheless strictly accurate. A rank, exuberant and rather wanton individualism has characterized our own variety of Syndicalism from the start.

In Europe intelligent Anarchists of the most pronounced type have been a part of the movement. In Spain (1908) they followed their leader Malatesta into the trade unions. Many of the French Syndicalists, like Pelloutier the founder, Delesalle, Pouget and Yvetot, glory in the anarchist name. Sorel, whom the academician, Paul Bourget, says is the most penetrating intelligence among Syndicalists, has neither hesitations nor concealments about this. He tells us plainly how great an event it was when Anarchists gained admission to the trade unions. "Historians," he tells us, "will one day recognize that this entrance was one of the greatest events which has happened in our time." In an eloquent passage he praises the work of the anarchist in the trade union, ending with the words. "They instructed labor that it need not blush for deeds of violence." I am fully aware how easy it is to take advantage of this scare word in order to make cheap points against the I. W. W. This pettiness may be avoided if we first state the truth. Anarchism, in its eviler aspects, is not in the least confined to the "lower classes." To flout and circumvent the law is anarchy, and none among our people have done this thing oftener, or on a larger scale, or with more effrontery, than many powerful business interests of the land. The Governor of California appointed a successful and highly respected business man to investigate and report upon the "disturbances in the city and county of San Diego," where the I. W. W. had become active as speakers on the street. On page 18 of this report, published by the state, may be seen editorial utterances of the two leading papers of San Diego, more wildly anarchistic than anything quoted from I. W. W. literature in this book. After very plain statements against the I. W. W., Colonel Weinstock reads the lesson (page 20) to the "good citizens" of San Diego:

"But it cannot now be said, nor will its good citizens say, when a normal condition shall be restored and sanity returns to the community, that there was any justification whatever on the part of men professing to be law-abiding citizens themselves to become law-breakers and to violate the most sacred provisions of the constitution; to preach with their mouths the sacredness of the constitution and its inviolability, and to break with their hands the most sacred provision of this same constitution by robbing men of their liberty; by assaulting them with weapons, by degrading and humiliating them, by endeavoring to thrust patriotism down their throats in compelling them with a weapon held over their heads to kiss the American flag, to sing the American national anthem and then to deport them."

From a citizen in lower California, I heard the defense of the "best men in San Diego." He was himself a prosperous man, of college training and of unusual public spirit; but the I. W. W. were "rats carrying a disease and were to be treated as such." They were to be treated as such "law or no law." "We could not," he said, "defend ourselves legally, and were morally justified in taking the law into our own hands." A college professor who was with me, tried to argue with him, saying, "But you, too, are defending the theory and practice of anarchy in its lowest form. You have at your back the whole accumulated machinery of laws and police powers that have been built up for the very purpose of putting an ordered and impersonal justice in the place of the old private codes. At the first strain, you fly to the old barbarisms." The gentleman was as unruffled as if a child had upbraided him. Through and behind his calm exterior one saw in darkened outlines too many probable conflicts between the anarchy of those who have and the anarchy of those who have not.

As far as I can learn, this caustic admonition is even more richly deserved by corresponding citizens in southern lumber camps. There have been dangerous approaches to the same fundamental lawlessness in recent dealing with this movement in many other communities.

It will be said, and rightly said, that this does not excuse a single outrage of I. W. W. origin. It does, however, put us in a frame of mind in which with some intelligent impartiality, we can judge the general spirit of anarchy in our midst. This may guard us from the moral poltroonery of forcing a standard upon the weak which the strong will not recognize or obey.

The element of anarchy peculiar to the I. W. W. is its inherent dislike of organic restraint. No one uses the word "organization" oftener or practices it less. All organization to be effective puts a curb upon its members. It standardizes conduct and sets definite limits to individual eccentricity, but the essence of anarchy is to reject group constraints. A century of trade unionism has brought about in its better membership a degree of organization that acts with great power upon individual whim and waywardness. Socialism has already acquired a great deal of organization that submits the individual to severe and continuous schooling. There are bickerings and wrangling enough in the socialist camps, but, at its best, it has established the fact of group-training which ranks it among the conserving social forces. Of the I. W. W. this cannot be said. It is held together by the yeasty dramatic commotions in which it is engaged. From its first convention eight years ago, it has been rent by temperamental dissensions. Such "organization" as it has, is a fitful and fluctuating quantity, ever ready to escape from the slightest real and steadying constraint which organization implies. Only by desperate efforts has the General Confederation in France held a minority membership that is always threatened by withdrawal of unions that have gained the least real stability.

To state the facts of this anarchistic tendency is not wholly to condemn the movement. It only defines its guerrilla character and its limitations. It only makes clearer to us what it is likely to do and what not to do.

There is not a spot where the Syndicalist fight has been waged in which the persisting and unavoidable conflict between the anarchistic and the social principle does not appear. An impetuous individualism cannot endure organic relationships.

In Italy if the tenant farm hands (mezzadria) wish to enter co-partnership with landlords and share the gains, the anarchist type in the movement wars against this, precisely as our I. W. W. attack all "labor contracts" or agreements with employers; precisely as they now fight the admirable "protocol" in the New York garment industry. These alliances with capitalism are an impediment to anarchist activity. With labor often less than thirty cents a day [1] and with the direct sympathy of small métayer farmers, the condition is perfect for Syndicalism, if it has developed the social as distinct from the anarchist feeling. Nowhere better than in Italy can we watch this conflict between the two types.

As the twentieth century came in, there were hundreds of strikes each year among these people. At the great agricultural strike in Italy with the help of Consul Jarvis at Milan, I saw the effects of this uprising. It was waged with incredible bitterness. On the industrial side, as in Milan, more than one hundred were shot and between two and three thousand imprisoned. As in our own western country, the authorities were paralyzed by numbers. Two years later King Humbert was murdered and it

[1] In 1898 I found men at work in the fields for 20 cents a day.

is a sinister comment that Syndicalists have made upon that event. The government relaxed its severities against "organizations," prompting such utterances as these: "Violence is said to be very wicked by the praying bourgeois, but we all now see that it is the only language to which the watch dogs of private property will listen. Let us not forget the lesson." Here is poverty with conscious discontent "that can be organized" into fighting trade unions. In northern industrial centers, the unions were federated into "Labor Bureaus." It was these latter (*Bourses du Travail*) in France that gave Pelloutier his chance to turn internal political feuds to his advantage and guide these federated bodies into the gathering current of revolutionary, anti-political Syndicalism with anarchist tendencies.

In Italy Anarchists proud of the title were prominent in the Labor Party at its formation in 1885. From this beginning, there never was a day's peace until six years later when Anarchists and Socialists separate because of incurable dissensions. The socialist is now the conservative; the "anarchist-syndicalist" is the revolutionary radical, shouting his contempt at every measure of "reform."

It seems to me to have the utmost significance that in this conflict, we see socialists in Italy within five or six years, shift their activities to the creation and strengthening of coöperative banks and distributive associations for the help of small farmers and wage earners. This was due in part to the growing conviction that small farming was not after all to be swallowed up, in any known time, by the big capitalistic culture. It was due still more, perhaps, to clearer understanding of the real issue between the logic of the Anarchist and that of the Socialist.

There is no chapter in the history of the labor struggle so luminously clear as that in which the practical Anarchist fights social organization. Wherever Socialism reaches the organic state, enabling it to coöperate with other social forces, the Anarchist attacks it as Bakounine attacked Marx, as Anarchists raised havoc with the Chartists and as W. D. Haywood is at this moment raising equal havoc with the socialist party.

This brings us to two rigorous tests to which Syndicalism must submit, if it is to pass out of activities primarily destructive. (1) How are the means of production to be taken over? (2) What proposals are given us for positive, constructive action?

XV

THE DISAPPEARANCE OF THE CAPITALIST

No practical question in the future of Socialism will excite more vehement controversy than that of "compensation." What Socialism wants and is determined to get is now largely possessed by what is loosely called the capitalist class. Like the ownership of land this control of the machinery of production is thought to give the possessors an almost unlimited power over the lives and destinies of those who are without property. It is this dependence and insecurity that accounts largely for the increasing hostility to the "wage-system." No analogy is so frequent as that of the slave relation under this system.

The remedy which Socialism brings is to get the land and all the vast mechanism embodied in transportation, mill, factory and mine away from its present holders. The people are themselves to own and use these wealth-producers in the common interest.

We shall see more clearly what the I. W. W. propose and also what they are likely to do, so far as they get power, if we dwell a moment on the more general attitude of socialism toward compensation.

If it is to take over "land and the means of production," it is fair to press the question: how is this to be done? There are plenty of socialists of conservative temper who reply that experience from a dozen countries furnishes all the answer we require. We have already "socialized" very considerable portions of "the means of production and of the land." In several countries this process has gone so far that the term "state socialism" accurately describes the stage of socialization already reached. No part of the "machinery of production" is so important as the railroad, yet it has been taken over in one country after another until the United States and England are almost alone among more than thirty countries to preserve private ownership. It is from English railway managers themselves that we now hear, "Our roads will be under government control within a few years. It is only a question of time." If we add to this history of socialized property, the telegraph, telephone and express companies, coal mines, life and fire insurance, trolley and gas systems, vast areas of public domain and forests, we get some measure of this process.

To the question, *how* is socialism to take possession, it is said, "We shall continue as we have begun. We have only to go straight on upon the same road, and long before the century is out we shall have every scrap of important business socialized."

Thus far, we see that these great private properties have been, upon the whole, fairly bought and paid for. There has been hardly an instance of confiscation. Even if railways, trolley and gas properties "originated in robbery," it is recognized that the properties have passed in large part to those who later bought in good faith. I have heard a socialist lecturer very eloquent on this point. "We should be," he said, "just as dirty thieves as the worst of them, not to take this immense transfer of property to innocent hands into account. Society has given every sanction that it can give to these acquisitions, and we don't propose to steal them."

When actual dispossession is necessary, a system of "bond issues to be paid out of profits in the industry" or various forms of "annuities" are proposed by many socialist writers.

There are most formidable financial difficulties connected with these proposals, but they put no affront on our sense of fair dealing. So far as we can believe that socialism, once in power, would "take over" the mills, mines and other industries with the same consideration toward present ownership, we could all look on unalarmed, except as we doubted the later results of such a policy.

If, then, socialism wins power enough, will the determining majorities vote as fairly as these soberer adherents now talk? That is not a frivolous inquiry. There are not merely "five-foot libraries," but ten-foot libraries filled with very different opinions as to how the great private properties are to be taken over. Socialists generally do not suggest taking them without "some" return. If for no other reason, they hesitate because of the practical political difficulties sure to attend an outright confiscation. "Even if right, it would not be politic," is a very common sentence. Very carefully the question of "how" is avoided by this large intermediate section. Again and again we read, "It must be left to the future;" "We will cross that bridge when we get to it;" which means that the dominating political opinion of that future will decide how little or how much shall be paid to present private holders of the desired "means of production." This tempered discretion of the " moderates " does not however exhaust ordinary socialist opinion. Long before we reach the audacities of the I. W. W. on this issue, we meet throngs of those in good party standing who make short shift of Fabyan prudencies. Among those who have dealt repeatedly and explicitly with this issue of compensation is Belfort Bax, a man of learning and one of the most prolific of socialist writers. In his volume on *The Ethics of Socialism* is a chapter on "Justice." It contains this passage, which I give with his own italics. After proving to his own satisfaction that the "means of production" to be taken over "are no longer in the hands of the producers," he says:

"Now, *Justice* being henceforth identified with *confiscation* and *injustice* with the rights of property, there remains only the question of 'ways and means.' Our bourgeois apologist admitting as he must that the present possessors of land and capital *hold* possession of them simply by right of superior force, can hardly refuse to admit the right of the proletariat organized to that end to *take* possession of them by right of superior force. The only question remaining is how? And the only answer is how you can. Get what you can that tends in the right direction, by parliamentary means or otherwise, *bien entendu*, the right direction meaning that which curtails the capitalist's power of exploitation. If you choose to ask further how one would like it, the reply is so far as the present writer is concerned, one would like it to come as drastically as possible, as the moral effect of sudden expropriation would be much greater than that of any gradual process."

Very coolly in his well-filled library he takes the logic of his own analysis. Capital secured its booty through force. *Injustice* is the name for present "rights of property." Justice will be restored when labor comes to its senses, taking from every proud cut-purse the treasures so long withheld from the labor that produced them. It is true that Jaurès, Kautsky, Bernstein, Shaw, the Webbs, H. G. Wells, and others who have international recognition, commit themselves to compensation—Bernstein and the Webbs most unequivocally—but close scrutiny of the other three who have commanding influence is perplexing. Jaurès writes: [1]

"We do not propose to adopt any violent or sudden measures against those whose position is now sanctioned by law, we are resolved, in the interests of a peaceful and harmonious evolution, to bring about the transition from legal injustice to legal justice with the greatest possible consideration for the *individuals* who are now privileged monopolists. We especially state that in our opinion it is the duty of the State to give an indemnity to those whose interests will be injured by the necessary abolition of laws contrary to the common good *in so far as this indemnity is consistent with* the interests of the nation as a whole."

These last words (the italics my own) are not without humor. Compensation "consistent with the interests of the nation as a whole," has to be interpreted by political majorities. The convenient elas-

[1] *Studies in Socialism*, p. 89.

ticity of his qualifying clause has the more significance because this greatest of socialist orators is reported to have said, as recently as 1906, in the Chamber of Deputies, that it was not possible to tell with certainty "Whether general expropriation of capitalistic property would be brought about with or without compensation." If his decision is finally against compensation, what torn shred would he leave to any arguing opponent begging the audience to adopt slower and more conservative measures?

Though Mr. Wells in his *New Worlds for Old* (p. 162) commits himself fervently to compensation and even insists that "property is *not* robbery," he has, like Jaurès, other moods. In his *Misery of Boots* he has this passage:

"And as for taking such property from the owners, why shouldn't we? The world has not only in the past taken slaves from their owners, with no compensation or with meager compensation; but in the history of mankind, dark as it is, there are innumerable cases of slave owners resigning their inhuman rights. . . . There are, no doubt, a number of dull, base, rich people who hate and dread socialism for purely selfish reasons; but it is quite possible to be a property owner and yet be anxious to see socialism come into its own. . . . Though I deny the right to compensation, I do not deny its probable advisability. So far as the question of method goes it is quite conceivable that we may partially compensate the property owners and make all sorts of mitigating arrangements to avoid cruelty to them in our attempt to end the wider cruelties of today."

In the heat of political appeal which of these two moods will prove the better vote getter?

If Mr. Wells himself before an audience were tilting with an adversary more "advanced" than he, what chances would his negative "advisability" get in the decision? First to deny the *right* to compensation and then with skittish half-heartedness, to talk about its "probable" advisability is to make easy work for the answering opponent.

More strictly of the Marx tradition, it is doubtful if any living writer carries more weight than Karl Kautsky. In the second part of *The Social Revolution* he is very explicit: "The money capitalist fulfills no personal function in the social life, and can without difficulty be at once expropriated. This will be all the more readily done as it is this portion of the capitalist class, the financier, who is most superfluous, and who is continually usurping domination over the whole economic life." The word "capitalist" is here used with precision as the receiver of interest. Like the landowner, as distinct from the working farmer, he is here held to be a parasite living off the laborer and has the same excuse for being as any other dead-beat. Why, then, should those holding such views consent to indemnify mere idlers? In the tug of politics, every extremist will show what real indemnity means. It means a huge issue of bonds thrown, as an interest-bearing debt, upon the people. Having been thoroughly instructed by socialism, that interest to private persons is theft, will they take kindly to this self-imposed burden, even if only during the life of the bondholder?

In our own country, there are few abler or more instructed socialist writers than Mr. Hillquit.   He is now under violent attack by the I. W. W. press and other revolutionaries as a "stoggy conservative," a "timid moss-back."   In his last book he thus states the case: [1]

"And similarly silent is the socialist program on the question whether the gradual expropriation of the possessing classes will be accomplished by a process of confiscation or by the method of compensation.   The greater number of socialist writers incline towards the latter assumption, but in that they merely express their individual present preferences.   Social development, and especially social revolutions, are not in the habit of consulting cut and dried theories evolved by philosophers of past generations, and social justice is more frequently a question of social expediency and class power.   The French clergy was not compensated for the lands taken from it by the bourgeois revolution, and the Russian noblemen and American slave owners were not compensated upon the emancipation of their serfs and chattel slaves.   It is not unlikely that in countries in which the social transformation will be accomplished peacefully, the state will compensate the expropriated proprietors, while every violent revolution will be followed by confiscation.   The socialists are not much concerned about this issue."

This writer has excellent legal training; has been a mayor's legal advisor in a considerable city.   In his analogies of the French clergy, Russian nobles and

[1] *Socialism.   In Theory and Practice*, 1910, p. 103.

American slave owners, and his closing assurance that socialists "are not much concerned about this issue," we may test with some fairness a far larger opinion than his own. Mr. Hillquit has served with distinction on the National Executive Committee of his party. That the I. W. W. should see in him so hopeless a conservative, gives us some hint of what this more revolutionary contingent would do with "methods of compensation."

A writer and teacher of deserved distinction, C. Hanford Henderson, writes his socialist book *Pay-Day*, to show why profit is theft. The motto on the fly leaf reads, "Thou shalt not steal;" but as the thieves have been the receivers of "profit," this moral warning cannot apply to those who are now to enter into possession of their own. Mr Henderson says, "The trust is a conscious violation of the Federal law. It is, moreover, built up out of stolen labor-power. On either count, the trust might with perfect justice and propriety be directly confiscated by the State. It is both contrabrand and stolen property." He concedes that this is "a harsh measure," and therefore tempers his surgery: "It might readily be enacted that any further transfer of stocks and bonds would be illegal and void, and that when the present owners died, the State should inherit their holdings. In this way the transfer from private to public ownership would be accomplished gradually and peacefully, without hardship to any actual owner of such securities. His heirs would, of course, be disappointed. But if it be granted that the living owner had no defensible right to such securities, it would be a sen-

timentalism to allow him to say what shall be done
with them after his death."

What, I ask, is it probable that popular majorities
would decide on the case as here presented? The property to be taken over was first gained in "conscious
violation of the Federal law." It is all "stolen labor-
power" and could be "confiscated by the State" with
"perfect justice." Could any eloquent foe of compensation have a better case than this? What would
one possessed of the passion of a great tribune do with
the hesitations and apologies of more conservative
men as they met in popular debate?

From the whole nebulous zone of wobbly socialist
opinions on compensation, we may now pass to the
I. W. W. where there is neither variableness nor shadow
of turning. There is little enough harmony in syndicalist ideas on many points, but that present capitalist possessors got their belongings through what in last analysis is fraud and force is a fixed and vehement belief.
"Are we then to pay market values or any values to
swindlers and highwaymen who have filched our properties?" One rarely hears a more effective gallery
stroke than this question, "Do you compensate pick-
pockets?" "Do you piously discuss financial methods
for recompensing the man who lifted your watch or
stole your bicycle?" I have many times listened to
discussions of this question of compensation before
general socialist audiences. "Shall capitalistic owners
be paid? If so, how much?" is one wording that I
heard discussed between conservative and radical
socialists. It was not because the radical had more
nimble wit or keener forensic ability; he caught and

held the applause because he forced home to the audience the popular logic of socialism: "If capitalism systematically robs us, why should we pay for what was never owned at all?" By so far as this belief is real, that labor has been fleeced, to that extent compensation is likely to fare ill.

It is not to be forgotten that socialists in control must decide their economic and administrative policies *politically*. Heads of departments must be politically chosen, fiscal and other measures likewise carried out by some form of majority vote.

I was told on the Alaska boat "Spokane" that Captain Carroll had a petition presented to him begging that some change of route be allowed. He replied, "Madame, this boat is not run by petition." That, under socialism, things are to be "democractically managed" is an accepted definition. Every question of "compensation" must be "democratically" determined. At popular gatherings opinion must be made then as it is now. Audiences must be warned and exhorted to vote for this or that measure. The last demagogue will not die with capitalism.

In an imagined picture of one of those future audiences discussing what should be paid to the owners of the last ripening "trust,"—which of two socialist speakers, one conservative and one radical, will have the surest hold upon the listening majority?

I do not press this as unanswerable, but it deserves reflection. In all democratic uprisings the easy advantage of the more radical man has been noted since Aristotle. Is it likely to be less so when the whole logic of democracy has become complete? I submit-

ted this to a thoughtful socialist now defending the
I. W. W. He replied that a generation or two of experience and better education would produce a democracy competent and self-restrained enough to deal
wisely and fairly with such issues as compensation.
This is possible, and we do well to entertain it as a
generous and admirable hope.

Meantime the I. W. W. are scoffingly impatient even
of these prudent qualifications. They tell us, "Capitalism is already ripe almost to rotting." Like a dead
substance, it is something from which we are to cut
ourselves loose. Both in precept and example they are
very specific. Their ablest exponents now state their
case in the monthly *International Socialist Review*. In
the last issue in my possession, a writer in the interest
of "Simplicity" puts the case as follows:

"The world's people belong to or support one of the
two great classes, capitalists or workers.

"What have we got? Nothing. What have they
got? Everything.

"Now we want it. Simple, isn't it?

"We demand all they've got. Why? Because they
have stolen it from us. We are the disinherited of the
earth and we are getting ready to take back what belongs to us.

"They told us in the beginning that there was a
chance for all. Now we know that they lied.

"We have become wise to the fact that we are the
victims, the suckers, the fallguys, in the greatest bunco
game ever invented. We put all we had into it—our
health, our hopes, our strength and power to labor—
but everything went merely to make them richer and

stronger. The result is that they are the owners of everything that makes life worth living.

"We want it back. Now how are we going to get it?

"Ask them for it? They would hand us the laugh.

"Buy it from them? It never belonged to them in the first place—no, we are going to take it.

"Take it how? By force? No, not necessarily. By bullets? We are not so foolish. We have the power already. We far outnumber them and our brains, when used, are as good as theirs. Therefore, we will organize our power and use our brains in our own behalf hereafter instead of theirs. When the workers are once solidly united the system by which the capitalists daily rob us of the fruits of our toil will simply fall of its own weight."

A leaflet, the *Noon Hour Chat*, sent out by the socialist section closest akin to the I. W. W. ends with these words:

"Precedents from American history are all against the theory of compensation to capitalist owners. The thirteen American colonies having asserted their independence had no scruples about 'confiscating' to themselves millions of acres of land hitherto vested in the British crown. The North had no scruples in confiscating property valued at one billion dollars, when it freed the chattel slave.

"Capitalism comes into court with dirty hands when it crys 'Confiscation!' From the time it unjustly confiscated the rights of the peasants in the land, down to our own time when it has virtually confiscated the entire wealth of the nation, and continuously confiscates in a variety of ways the property of the middle class, capitalism has one long record of rapine, bloodshed and wholesale theft.

"The verdict of the court, of the working class, organized and aware of its mission, that will yet thunder forth to capitalism will be: Restore to us, the People, that which is rightfully ours and which you have stolen.

"There will be no 'compensation' about it. Such is the answer of the Socialist Labor Party." [1]

Here owners and non-owners stand over against each other as robbers and robbed. Labor, the creator of wealth, has "Nothing." Capitalistic owners have "Everything." Therefore labor demands "all they have got." "Why? Because they have stolen it from us." We are left in doubt about the use of " force " in this transfer. It may not be " necessary." Labor once " solidly united " will find that the whole capitalistic system " will simply fall of its own weight."

From observations submitted in the last chapter, the conclusion is fairly safe that these brisk iconoclasts will not have their way. They will not have it, because so many of the working class have too much at stake. They will not have it, because it will be seen to be neither fair nor safe. They will not have it, because other methods are now slowly appearing through which the evils of capitalism can be met with decency and good faith.

Before the century is out, ways will be found, largely through more intelligent taxation, to squeeze

[1] This is to be sharply distinguished from the Socialist Party.

out enormous reserves of unearned increment. This reasoned policy is a working part of the advanced social politics in so many countries as to offer a more honorable escape from "the armored inequalities" against which the protest comes.

XVI

CONSTRUCTIVE SUGGESTION

WE have seen that Syndicalists have lost faith in the halting legalities of political and reform action. They move straight upon the enemy. They say bluntly that the capitalist and present business managers are incompetent for their work. In an article by an English Syndicalist, which I have twice seen quoted in our I. W. W. literature, occurs this passage:

"Leave us, you 'captains of industry,' if you cannot manage the industries so as to give us a living wage and security of employment. Go! if you are so short-sighted and so incapable of coming to a common understanding among yourselves, that you rush like a flock of sheep into every new branch of production which promises you the greatest momentary profits, regardless of the usefulness or noxiousness of the goods you produce in that branch! Go, if you are incapable of building your fortunes otherwise than by preparing interminable wars, and squandering a good third of what is produced by every nation in armaments for robbing other robbers. Go! if all that you have learned from the marvelous discoveries of modern science is that you see no other way of obtaining one's well-being but out of that squalid misery to which one-third of the population of the great cities of this extremely wealthy country are condemned. Go! and 'a plague o' both your houses' if that is the only way you can find to manage industry and trade. We, workmen, will know better how to organize production, if we only succeed in getting rid of you, the capitalist pest!"

Capitalists can still make profit for themselves and their friends, but the disenchanted Syndicalist denies that this is "good business." He will call no business "good" that does not enrich the people as a whole. This is his measure of "ability" and there is much to be said for this view. The really able man will so conduct affairs as to help others as much as himself. Capitalism it is said, now in its decadence, makes this inclusive service less and less possible. Labor must therefore itself take over the job.

The actual industry to be chosen is a question of time, place and practical expediency, but the *idea* becomes plain in the Post Office strike in Paris in 1910, while the practice has actual embodiment in specific coöperative triumphs now among our proved experiences. No one has better stated this idea in its highest expression than the Syndicalist, Odon Por. He seems to assume that years of trade union discipline with a developed "class-conscious" sense, must precede even an intelligent plan of operation. It is assumed that the unions have passed through the guerrilla stage of strikes, learning both their strength and weakness. In his words: "When the workers have attained the highest technical skill and efficiency; when they are able and ready actually to run their industries, ready with their perfected organization and their skilled professional individuality, they will then take them over." When I asked an I. W. W.

lecturer what business in the United States would
answer to the above condition, he replied that our
railroads already had unions, with technical knowledge enough among engineers and in the shops to take
over and run the system " within a very few years."
He thought the Western Federation of Miners already
equipped to run the mines and that the big breweries
had a labor organization powerful enough and technical equipment so advanced that they might easily
pass from capitalist to labor management. Much of
the electrical work he believed to be in the same
hopeful stage of transition.

He made much of the familiar suggestion that the
general trust development had proved already that
the biggest business can be run by those who have
developed within the business and are hired by the
outside capitalist. "If they will do it for the capitalists, they will do it for all of us." To the redoubtable
question as to how these enterprises were to be
financed, he replied that a few years more of increasing unrest, strikes becoming more and more general,
interspersed with the gaieties of sabotage, would make
capitalistic investments so uncertain and insecure
that the outside capitalist would tire of the game.
"The financier," he said, "does not realize in the
least how hard we are going to make it for him to run
these things in the old way."

According to Odon Por it is a great step toward the
new order that the clerical force in the French Post
Office has lost confidence in the official political management. In his own words: "The employees were
tired of being directed and dominated by a political

department administered by politicians who had no comprehension of the work of the Post Office clerk, nor indeed of the work in general." The department can now be better run "without officials retained at high salaries, holding their positions because of political influence, though destitute of the least expert knowledge of the business." Everything that concerns the Post Office is known by the total body of workers who now carry it on. Why then should the entire management be refused them?

The Syndicalist argues against "throwing the railways into politics," as briskly and confidently as the average American business man. He has only contempt for Government ownership as now practiced. To these revolutionaries, the railroad in possession of any present government may be as viciously capitalistic as in private hands, besides being badly managed. Italy has taken over the roads and so badly bungles them as to rouse the same jeers, according to Odon Por, as in the case of the French Post Office. He says a very powerful Industrial Union is now established on government roads. These include practically all except the more highly paid officials. Of the aim of this Union, he says:

"By its method of organizing according to the technical nature of each man's occupation, while the problems of the whole service are kept before the mind of every member and his opinion and vote called for on each, the men are educated to a keen interest in everything that concerns the whole work of the railways. That they have arrived at a considerable degree of success is proved by the fact that, conscious of their increased collective power, they set before themselves the revolutionary aim—'*The Railways for the Railwaymen.*'

He adds: "The technical incompetence of the bureaucratic administration has demoralized the system and brought about a growing yearly deficit in the returns. Innumerable sinecures and well-paid offices were established; but the State neglected the technical side, and with increased financial burden came greater confusion in the working.

"On the other hand, through their organization the workers have been eagerly learning details of every kind of work necessary for the proper effective managing of the railways, and now they seek to get control over their administration, so as to manage the railways for the nation. They propose to do this as a coöperative society, which would be made up of the members of their union. . . ."

He quotes conservative economists of world-wide reputation and experts such as Professor Vilfredo Pareto who have declared that the one practical solution of the trouble is, since private ownership is a public nuisance, and state ownership a veritable disaster, to entrust the State railways to the coöperative enterprise of the organized railway-men. It is further maintained that the State has taken the first step toward this end in its law of 1911, which opens the way for a partnership with the unions, so far as to give their own elected representatives a voice in management. "The Government," he says, "thus proved its recognition of the fact that it cannot run the railway industry efficiently without the direct coöperation and advice of the employees."

Thus far we have to do with the syndicalist purpose and idea. Through the word "coöperative" we pass from the idea to its proposed applications in practice. This constructive suggestion touches anarchistic and communist ideals long familiar to us. These seek to develop local autonomous groups, federated "as necessity arises," but united in their loathing of a centralized bureaucratic State. These decentralized activities are to preserve for the individual "the utmost freedom consistent with conditions set by these voluntary associations."

This suggestive idealist counts upon the renaissance of democratic coöperation to further this end. He illustrates it by two instances, one in industry and the other upon the land:

"The Bottle Blowers' Industrial Union of Italy has discovered the material, technical, commercial, and moral capacities for getting hold, within a comparatively short period of time, of the biggest share of the Italian bottle industry, and sooner or later it will undoubtedly run the whole industry through its co-operatives."

"The force which these workers have substituted for individual and associated capitalist initiative, namely, the collective effort and efficiency of their organized class, foreshadows to Syndicalists the future, with its economic progress and continuously growing moral improvement."

In agriculture, the basic industry of Italy, the same factors are at work on a much larger scale. Here he tells us some 200,000 acres have passed into the hands of the farm laborers organized into unions and coöperative societies. Through industrial organizations and Socialist education the agricultural laborers acquired the power, the technical capacity, and the moral energies to fight for, obtain, and run their industry.

These last lines contain the gist of these winged hopes. Through the technical and moral development of the trade union, labor is to enter into possession of one important industry after another. It is to do this by proving its technical and moral superiority over capitalism already dying before our eyes.

We here have the syndicalist view of the laborer as the creating unit that lives and has his being inside the machinery of production. He is in the mine, factory, shop, ship, and bank. Here his skill and faculty develop. On this basis his trade union is to rest. It is the primary industrial cell. It is to be built into federations with delegates that shall represent the whole industrial life. To the minutest part these, and these only, know the process through which foods, stuffs, metals, are made. It is these real creators who also carry all products to the consumer. Here, then, should be the seats of power. What is now called politics will be remade. With the workers once enthroned, politics will express the administrative necessities of the new order in which "none shall live except by work." Youth, age, infirmity, shall be cared for, as under socialism, by direct appropriations from the social product. But investments, interest, profits, rent, and all inheriting of these values, are to be stopped, in order that loafers, rich and poor alike, shall have an end.

In the syndicalist vision coöperative groups furnish the higher efficiencies before which the private profit-maker can no longer hold his own. The capitalist is to be crowded out because of inefficiency and this can be shown through the object lessons which coöperation now offers.

I have dealt at length with this writer, because no one known to me has put the case with more coherence or on the same high level. If we can accept him as authoritative spokesman, there is no more danger in his proposals than in a new kind of Sunday school or a new breakfast food. We have only to watch and satisfy ourselves that his trade unions "functioning through coöperation," really display the superiorities claimed for them. If they should perform their various services with higher social benefit they are surely not to be feared.

It is true that many European cities have found distinct advantages in letting out various kinds of work—like paving, drainage, printing—to coöperative groups. Italy has produced a type of self-organizing gang electing its own foreman and doing job-work (in which the labor cost is high) coöperatively. Hundreds of these have proved so successful that Government and cities give them preferential advantages. The Societies are registered and work in small gangs. As elsewhere, experiment has shown that discipline becomes too difficult with larger numbers. One often finds the coöperative store affiliated with this working plan. The profits of each gang go to no outsider, but automatically to themselves when the job is done. They have built city slaughter houses and made whole streets in Parma. The Minister Luzzatti gave them his active sympathy and helped them to the uses of the coöperative banks, of which he was founder.

Is there here the germ from which the future Commonwealth may spring? Taken together with many thousands of other coöperative forms in agriculture, banking, distribution and production, it offers the fairest hopes for the democratic management of business that actual experience can show. Ordinary "State Socialism" is much less democratic than the free activities of workingmen's coöperation.

What charms "the higher syndicalism" in coöperation is that it eliminates the master. The Italian "braccianti" and "muratori" have no boss except of their own electing. If they need a technical engineer, he comes as their fellow counsellor and peer, never as a "boss." The gang substitutes its own supervision for that of an employer and also takes the risks. If one can imagine the world's chief business done through such voluntary groups, they would displace the bureaucratic State hated by all Syndicalists.

In this manner, Kropotkin's shining dream would be fulfilled. In loosely federated groups, men and women would do their work like artists and men of science. There would be no enslaving trusts, but "small factories and upon the land, such intensive culture as science now makes possible." This thought has long hovered in the minds of Anarchists of the Kropotkin type.[1]

[1] As this goes to press, G. P. Putnam's Sons publish a cheap up-to-date edition of Kropotkin's *Fields, Factories and Workshops* in which this faith in the "decentralization of industries;" the "combination of industry and agriculture" has the most intelligent and inspiring expression yet given it.

Even in our country, as early as 1883, it appeared in anarchist "Principles," the second, third, and sixth articles of which read as follows:

"Establishment of a free society based upon co-operative organization of production.

"Free exchange of equivalent products by and between the productive organizations without commerce and profit-mongery.

"Regulation of all public affairs by free contracts between the autonomous (independent) communes and associations resting on a federalistic basis."

Neither in the literature nor in many conversations, have I ever got the slightest convincing intimation as to how these "loosely federated unions" are to work in the indispensable exchange of products in the world market, The highly trained expert, we are told, is to play a great part. These skilled persons in the various industries are to "represent" such social organization as exists. This revives an idea on which publicists have speculated for a half century— "representation by interests,"—schoolmasters, manufacturers, farmers, miners, etc., each to choose its own representative. It is a conception, if largely conceived, which points to a possible political structure of far higher order, but nothing could so surely defeat it as the fighting methods of Syndicalism based on the "class war" as conceived by American Syndicalists. The harsh aggressiveness with which our I. W. W. insist upon this leaves every constructive feature almost a burlesque.

For example, on the basis of Trautmann's pamphlet, *One Big Union,* a chart has been drawn of the future industrial system. It generously includes the entire globe, thus opening new floodgates for more merciless competition. It will have nothing to do with lines that separate states or nations. The plan has four great departments:

(1) Agriculture and Fisheries.
(2) Manufacture and Production.
(3) Mines.
(4) Construction.

Each of these is subdivided—the first into stock and farming, horticulture, forestry, and fisheries; mining into those who work in coal and coke, oil and gas, metals, salt, sulphur, stone, and gems; the two others likewise with more minute sub-divisions. At the center is the seat of Administration and Communication from which radiate to the circumference the divisions of Public Service and Transportation, with all the activities, including electric, gas, and water supplies; education, health, marine and air navigation. Here we have the basis of labor organization which will "correctly represent the working class." It combines all wage-workers "in such a way that it can most successfully fight the battles and protect the interests of the working people of today in their struggle for fewer hours, more wages and better conditions." It also offers "a final solution of the labor problem—an emancipation from strikes, injunctions, bull-pens and scabbing of one against the other."

We are told finally to "observe how this organization will give recognition to control of shop affairs, provide perfect Industrial Unionism, and converge the strength of all organized workers to a common center, from which any weak point can be strengthened and protected.

"Observe, also, how the growth and development of this organization will build up within itself the structure of an Industrial Democracy—a Workers' Coöperative Republic—which must finally burst the shell of capitalist government, and be the agency by which the workers will operate the industries, and appropriate the products to themselves.

"One obligation for all.

"A union man once and in one industry, a union man always and in all industries.

"Universal transfers.

"Universal emblem.

"All workers of one industry in one union; all unions of workers in one big labor alliance the world over."

All this is to be done by creating a sense of solidarity among all the labor units. Every selfish trade union is to lose itself in a larger whole. Because men work in glass or leather, they are not to call their unions after the tools or products used. " Agriculture, for example, would gather into one union."

"All farm workers, in plowing, planting, reaping, and fertilizing operations—which would, of course, include all engineers, firemen, blacksmiths, repair-workers, carpenters, etc., working on farms and engaged in farm-product work. All workers on cotton and sugar plantations would come into this group, also all irrigation-workers, that is, all working at the operation of irrigation-systems as engineers, pumpmen, lockmen, pipe and repairmen, etc. On cattle and live stock farms: ranchmen, herders, sheep shearers, general utility men, all workers on fowl and bird farms; on dairy farms, etc."

Again the Department of Civil Service and Public Conveniences contains:

(A) Hospitals and sanitariums.
(B) Sanitary protective division.
(C) Educational institutions.
(D) Water, gas and electricity supply service.
(E) Amusement service.
(F) General distribution.

This would merge scores of craft unions that had been built up on sectional interests. Against this "curse of sectionalism" the Syndicalist acts.

It is a curse because it cultivates a selfish monopoly spirit. "One Big Union" in each industry, ever ready to unite with those in other industries, is the remedy. With this perfected solidarity once attained, labor has only to *stop*, and the catastrophe of capitalism is at hand. This may be done playfully with smiling lips and hands in pockets.

What Mr. Trautmann's pamphlet has done is to give us a blurred caricature of present commercial activities in the world.[1] This is done apparently to show pictorially how easily the "world brotherhood of labor" may be instructed to oust the present possessors.

From Sir Thomas More to William Morris, we have nothing more soaringly utopian than that which this

[1] I am told that in the Sixth Convention this chart has now been "entirely made over." In the I. W. W. *Solidarity*, Nov. 30, 1912, is a long and critical article on necessary changes.

chart furnishes. It implies heights and depths of organization of which our present despised "state bureaucracy" scarcely gives us a hint. It implies a system of representation and a politics on a scale far beyond anything which now exists. If this charted dream were to be Utopia (that is, "Nowhere"), one would greet it on its own terms, but the I. W. W. are above all bent on things practical. All circuitous ways, as through politics and parliaments, are not for them. It is "action" that educates and action that frees labor from its chains. Capitalism is now so far gone that its dissolution needs only to be hastened by "direct action," sabotage, the strike in every phase,— local, short, and quick, sympathetic,—and finally the general uprising.[1]

The childlike simplicity of this proposal astonishes us the more because it seems to be here recognized, that as the world is bound closer and closer together, exchange of products must go on; that kinds, amounts, terms of exchange, have in some way to be determined, and that all this can only be through boards chosen by the various trades. As "the Globe itself is to be one brotherhood," international affil-

[1] The most recent statement by the general secretary of the order reads:

"All power vests in the general membership through the initiative and referendum and the right of repeal and recall.

"Universal transfer system and recognition of cards of union workers of all countries; one initiation fee to be all that is required, and this is to be placed at such a figure that no worker will be prevented from becoming a union man or woman because of its amount.

"A universal label, badge, button and membership card, thus promoting the idea of solidarity and unity amongst the workers.—*Solidarity*, Jan. 18, 1913."

iations are to be more fluid and intimate than ever.

That the "point of production" and the product are to be made the new basis of reconstruction, does not free us an atom from red-tape complications involved in the amount of organization absolutely necessary to the administrative toil incident to the management of a world market by the "Grand Assembly composed of delegates from National Unions."

It is unthinkable that these bodies can work except through committees entrusted with large powers. It is as unthinkable that these powers can be exercised without large authority and a good deal of permanence of tenure in office.

In distant industries, will those restless minorities, which appear wherever human beings congregate, submit to such authority without the factional resistance which even now plagues the I. W. W. to the point of breaking? There is even less warrant for such hope because Syndicalism rests so confidently and so exclusively on economic and business interests. These are not primarily the harmonizing, brother-making forces in the world.

There is a sentence in some early Christian writer that reads: "We believe because it is impossible." Of this portion of the I. W. W. belief we can say no less. It is a naïve faith which restores again an almost forgotten theology. It awaits a Day of Judgment (for capitalism) as breathlessly as its predecessors. "Predestination" never had a more perfervid utterance in spite of clamorous approval of Mr. Bergson. Never was the poor old world more sharply divided into black and white, sheep and goats, God and Devil, Heaven and Hell than in this philosophy.

We are offered here a conception of economic relations which necessarily raises impossible questions and still more impossible "solutions."

The disciplined and soberest element in the socialist movement, as well as in the older trade unions, already sets problems and presses them for solution, which will tax to the limit all the strength and intelligence at our command. Trade unions, for example, are generally thought to be ridiculous in assuming some sort of "right to the job" that has been deliberately abandoned in a strike. The absurdity of this "right" is so clear in the case of the individual who leaves his employer, that we think it safe to apply the principle to collective action. Yet recent years have shown in several countries that mass-action in strikes may assume proportions and at the same time get strategic control over the sources of social safety, that raise problems on which the individual instance throws no ray of light.

This illustration shows by comparison, the intrepid lengths to which I. W. W. claims are pressed. "Of course the job is ours! Whose is it if not ours?" says one of them. "It is ours as much when we are out as when we are in."

But this is simplicity itself compared to the next step. Not only does the job belong to them, but the tools, machinery, mill and industry itself. "All these are ours because we laborers made them." Scores of times I have heard this preached with placid innocence, the depths of which no doubting appeal to the speaker could in the least disturb.

After a lecture on some phase of labor troubles, a young lady, who had been nettled by some remark, made tart objections. "My father," she said, "employs hundreds of men. They make no end of trouble for him, though he gives every one of them a living." She had at her tongue's end the exact amounts which went each week to "support," as she said, these troublesome employees. When I ventured to ask if it was really so onesided as that: if the men in the factory did not also help "support" her father: if they gave him nothing in return for all his favors, I found, though she had college training, that the question had no meaning for her. She was going about in her little world carrying in her pretty head this dense illusion that her father was a kind of patron saint dispensing favors to ungrateful and little deserving mill hands.

Years after, at a strike against another kind of mill, I met a youth to whom Syndicalism was a religion. With glowing sincerity he was telling the packed hearers about him that the employers were "shirkers and not workers." "They did not make that mill or anything in it. From cellar to roof labor made it; and what labor makes, labor should have."

Here again was the young lady. As with her, I tried to draw from him some further statement about the employer's obvious part in the creation and maintenance of the mills in question. But this meant nothing to him. There was no further question in his mind. "The mill is ours and we shall take our own."

Since then, these two have hung in my memory as companion pictures. In point of density, one illusion is as pernicious as the other. There are views so

wildly unrelated to any possible social change, that we
rightly set them down among the antics of a disordered
or undisciplined mind.   An I. W. W. writer has com-
plained in one of their journals that too many of the
membership enter upon oratorical instruction before
they are in the least prepared for it.   He then adds:
"These new converts are too much 'in advance'
to be of any help to the cause," but how can one
ignorant of his own business be "in advance" of
anything?   Why not state it as it is.   "They are so
far behind that they are unfit to teach."   A nimble
vanity is not confined to certain criminal and degen-
erate types.   It has the thriftiest growths in that
immaturity which first peeps in upon some vast
human problem and is at once fired to suffocation with
desire to lift the burden of the world's ignorance.   It
is always the mark of this immaturity to assume that
its light burns far in advance of the dull and lagging
multitude.   If these old fogy survivals mock or turn
deaf ears, the neophyte finds easy solace in the
thought that other great light-bearers of the race have
met the same hard fate.   I once heard the ironic
pleasantry, "Don't try to reform the world until you
are perfectly certain that the world can't reform *you*."
Such reproof as the rebuke carries has a far wider
application than to I. W. W. neophytes.   It applies
to every shade of crude impatience from which few
of us are wholly free.

On a far higher plane is the constructive suggestion
of Odon Por.   It is full of speculative charms but,
at every point, fatal to the benumbing practices of
our I. W. W.

No movement commits itself to coöperation without at the same time committing itself to the peaceful and creative methods of reform. Workmen's coöperation has a growth of two generations. There is not a spot where it has won the least real power that it has not affiliated with politics and with reforms. This is both its hope and its strength. It grows only by creative action. Sabotage and strikes alike are an abomination to the coöperator. His success is measured by his achievements in substituting an efficiency superior to that of private profit-making employers. He deliberately enters into competition with them to prove that certain middlemen are useless and therefore parasitic.

This high and strenuous task leaves no time for the "organized delays of sabotage." So far as Syndicalism turns to coöperation, it falls into line with the world's best and safest reform work.

No one assures of this with more impressiveness than the "intellectual father" of the movement, George Sorel. It is not merely that he rejects sabotage, he rejects even more all attempts to chart off the future of society. His interest is in the obscure, unconscious forces which underlie this mass-movement. He sees the middle class in a state of decay. All the commanding energies through which, for centuries, it came to power have sickened. It is to him a thing for pity and contempt. If a spark of hope is left for the bourgeois, it can only be kindled by the breath of revolution.[1] This leads him to exalt the possibilities

[1] See the brilliant and impartial analysis in the first chapters of *La Philosophie Syndicaliste*, by George Guy-Grand.

of violence. It has the serpent's charm to fix the eye upon its object. Militant English women drop their pruderies, attack persons and property. The nation gasps, but sits up and pays attention. The cause gets a hearing. To Sorel no great social uprising is possible without drama. The imagination must be shocked and fascinated. The Reformation, the Revolution of 1789, the Italian revolt against Austria, owed their successes to this spectacle of daring and uncalculating action.

It is neither important nor relevant to ask if this violence is "good" or "moral." It is justified if it is efficient; if it works toward its end in getting things done. Wherever these forces gain such headway as to shift power from one class to another, we have the essence of a "Revolution," the soul of which is religion. This religion of social insurgency is Myth, but to him that lessens neither its power nor its sanctity. It has not the slightest consequence that the myth is not "true." It is true in the sense that Napoleon's victories were won by aid of myths with which his soldiers clothed their leader.

These metaphysical rhapsodies are not from the pen of a literary trifler. They are the serious reflections of a highly trained engineer whose intellectual gifts have left their impress upon some of the best minds of our time. They are ideas, however, very awkward for all those who make charts of any society built on the ruins of the present order. The disgust which the socialist poet Morris felt for Bellamy's Utopia would be as nothing to Sorel's repulsion for the whole constructive mechanism within which Mr. Trautmann and others frame their future society.

In the critical objections of this chapter there is no word of denial that our I. W. W. may upon other grounds justify their existence. They may be honestly accounted for because of things intolerable in our present disorders. Syndicalism, with its excesses of statement and of action, with all the fantasm of its working method will continue, and *should* continue as one among other prodding annoyances that leave society without peace until it dedicates far more unselfish thought and strength to avoidable diseases like unmerited poverty, unemployment, grotesque inequalities in wealth possession, the forced prostitution of underpaid women, and our fatuous brutalities in dealing with crime.

To accept these and kindred social sicknesses as fatalities is as excuseless as to accept tuberculosis or hookworm as permanent and unavoidable ills.

XVII

SOME EFFECTS OF RESPONSIBILITY

THE larger world area, from which Syndicalism sprang, on which it has developed and now acts, must be studied, not merely for its origins, but to learn what fate has befallen it; what internal and external difficulties have appeared.

This natural history of the movement in very different countries will enable us to make a closer estimate of its possible destinies in the United States. That a very few years of revolutionary activity in France, for example, should produce an inner schism in which radical and conservative Syndicalists confront each other as in opposing camps instructs us because we see the same beginnings and the same tendency already among our I. W. W. The explanation is almost too simple to be stated. In any large gathering of bread winners, many are married, others want to be; some are well paid and have continuous work, others are ill paid for fitful and uncertain jobs, some are sceptical of revolutionary methods, others are so far satisfied with their wages as to prefer them to doubtful chances. These actual and temperamental differences inevitably come to the surface. Those who are permanently led by the power of a distant and uncertain ideal are few, while those are many who, soon or late, yield to the pressure of the nearer need. This conflict in the estimate of interests shattered the Knights of Labor. It may not shatter our I. W. W., but it will constantly check it, producing from within, its own conservative reactions. These are now so distinct in France that the words, "lefts," "rights," and "moderates," are seen in the recent literature. There are not only "reformists" (conservatives) like Niel, Keufer, Renard and Albert Thomas, but there are trade union groups that bear the same name. Steady and fairly remunerative work holds them back from hazardous ventures. Each of the above men has borne the heavy responsibilities attached to the office of working secretary, Keufer of the printers, Renard of the textile workers.[1] In their positions things have to be done and not merely talked about or shirked by passing resolutions. Even if the wage system is outworn, the actual present facts of that system have now to be faced, as do the other conditions of sanitation, wages and hours of labor. The struggle with these hard realities begets the cooler temper and soberer choice of ways and means. Even Socialism that has borne its responsibilities is lined up against capitalism as unflinchingly as the I. W. W. Both desire to capture the power now held by capitalists, but the tactics differ about as widely as hot impulse differs from cool reflection. Yet the I. W. W. change their attitude wherever the struggle passes into the stage of definite accountabilities. When we are wiser we shall meet them at this point. It is precisely in that situation that education—for them and for us—is possible.

---

[1] As early as 1904, in the *Mouvement Socialist* (November) an attack upon this more cautious membership was made by the anarchist Pouget.

In the resounding victory which the I. W. W. claim at Lawrence, the very success forced its petty compromises with employers and with the wage system, closely after the manner of ordinary trade union dickering. Instead of "No compromise with employer or with wage-slavery," there was the same opportunist give-and-take. Superintendents were waited upon, and others of the strike committee held counsel with Boston officials of the American Company, to argue out the demands for fifteen per cent advance, discontinuance of the premium system and extra pay for overtime. This is the world-old story—the quick reaction of responsibility upon behavior. As it falls upon the I. W. W., the leaders begin to substitute some degree of cautious calculation for impulsive action. This reverses much eloquent theorizing upon the vices of the reason and the virtues of instinct which marks so much syndicalist speculation. When urgent and conflicting duties face us for immediate decisions, every conscious and rational faculty must act.

On the first approach of definite responsibility the I. W. W. reflect, compare and balance. They act as the politician acts. In the high flights of agitation, demands are sweeping and all things promised. "There shall be no compromise with the wage system because it is robbery," are words I heard from a speaker in the Lawrence strike. But on the first assurance that the battle was to be won, compromise was a necessity. With as much shrewdness as haste, the strikers took to the ordinary bartering of practical men. As the theory passed into a situation that must be met, they met it in the spirit of a sensible trade union or an arbitration board:—the spirit of a wholesome opportunism.

On wing in the "oratorical zone" they will stand upon "principle," will have the whole loaf or none. Face to face with the fact, they take their slice like the most despised of reformers. They are delighted to get for the skilled a slice so thin as a rise of five per cent, and to shout over the victory. In motive at least, it is much to their credit that the lowest paid should have the highest increase. The discrimination against the rewards of skill is open to grave question, but it is one of their "principles" to which much fidelity has been shown. They will, however, as others, take what they can get. They will haggle for this in ways as ancient as exchanges on a far Eastern market.

If their power grows, the old opportunist method will keep pace with it driving the wedge deeper between the Anarchist and those who accept the limitations and power of organization.

At the present writing an I. W. W. Proclamation goes out from Pittsburg to all steel, iron and coke workers in the district. It begins: "The hour has arrived.—Tie up all the mills, shut down the mines, blow out the furnaces and the ovens, pull the fires, stop the engines and the pumps—strike, strike all, hear ye, all together to win."

The demand reads:

THE EIGHT-HOUR WORKDAY

In all steel and iron mills and factories, in all mines, in the coke districts, everywhere!

AN INCREASE OF 40 PER CENT

in wages for the workers receiving less than $2 per day,
of 20 per cent for all receiving from $2 to $4 per day,
and a 5 per cent increase for all receiving more than
$4 per day.

"Time and a half for overtime, double time for work
on holidays."

All this is not a reproach. It shows good sense.
But it shows also that the struggle instantly develops
exigencies which divide men on the tactics to be employed. With every extension of the struggle, with
every new increment of power and the liabilities it
brings, these practical tactics make sharper division
among those upon whom the burdens fall. Thus the
struggle becomes selective and the process increases
with every new committee to which special tasks are
assigned. Every step involves organization, but this
is intolerable to the Anarchist. Organization imposes
delays, uniformities, and restraints. Within it the
individual cannot do as he likes. One Syndicalist
says, "Our history is nothing but the Fourth Estate
coming to consciousness and thus to power." The
Revolution of 1848, he says, was the final signal of
victory. Out of it came the "World Brotherhood,"
the International of 1863. But organization with its
fixing of responsibilities and limitations was found
necessary even in the International.

As organization developed and coöperative action
and conciliation in team-work became necessary, the
eternal conflict with the anarchist type set in, as it will
in all syndicalist and socialist fellowship.

Why, in its first heroic effort to bring the workers of the world together, did the International run amuck? It was not from any external opposition but solely from its own inner strife and discord. It could unite on the great phrases, but at the first attempt to construct policies the war was on. The war was on, moreover, precisely as it is now on between the I. W. W. on one side, and the American Federation of Labor, together with all of our more disciplined Socialists, on the other.

What drove the International from pillar to post was the presence of the Anarchist. The Anarchist refuses to submit to "group discipline." His name for the Devil is any sort of authority outside himself. For temporary shifts he will form a group, but the individual is not held by it.

He is continually slipping out of the restraining group and playing his hand alone after his own temperament. This, in the field of action, is the essence of anarchy.

For almost twenty years the International struggled with this outlaw element until the Association was driven to New York city, where it staggered on for a few years under the guidance of Johann Most.

The trade unions were of course first to discover the impossibility of working with this body. Then, one by one, it was abandoned by socialist groups. In this short history, we actually find the Anarchists themselves splitting into three warring sections each with its own emphasis.

One of these (Anarchist-Communist) splits again over the question of violence—when, where and how much violence may be sanctioned?

Twenty-five years ago we had the I. W. P. A. (International Working People's Association) and the I. W. A.; the latter claiming that "violence should be held in more restraint."

This same turbulent history will repeat itself in our own I. W. W., as it struggles with the older unionism and with that part of our Socialism which affiliates with political action and reform.[1]

It is this strife between extreme individualism, or small recalcitrant minorities, and political majorities which produce all "reformist" parties that one sees now powerfully at work in France.

Syndicalism of the "reformist" character vetoes every extreme proposal of the revolutionary branch. First and most fundamental, it distrusts the action of small minorities as it rebels against giving the same vote to a small union as to a large one.[2] It insists upon steadying the movement by appeal to entire federated groups. It asks, like the older unions, for more dues, more funds and benefits. It is less "anti-patriotic." It is far wiser about the possibilities of politics. It is

[1] In the organ of *Industrial Unionism* printed in Glasgow (December issue) the question is put: "Why is it that after about seven years of strenuous propaganda, and the sacrifice of time, money, and energy, the Industrial Union movement has failed to influence the working class?" In the January number, this is denied, but with evidence that proves the factional hostilities already at work. See *The Socialist* (Dec. and Jan.), 1912–13.

[2] This exercise of power by small minorities is so insultingly undemocratic that one is not surprised to find frequent bitter attacks on the "fetish of democracy."

not afraid of pension funds, and those like the printers, who have sick and strike funds, are in the "reformist" branch in France. Vigorous sections of textile, mine, tobacco workers and even railroad men are definitely reformist. The revolutionaries fight these cautious measures for the obvious reason that they are one and all the natural basis of agreements with employers' associations or with current political reforms. Such history of the syndicalist General Federation as is accessible shows clearly that a small and energetic minority hate the referendum appeal to large majorities. A leading "Reformist," A. Keufer, has from the start fought for the "collective contract," which assumes coöperation with employer and with politics.

All this inner struggle raises the question—Can Syndicalism develop permanent and constructive energies? This is inconceivable unless it affiliate with the main currents of existing social and reform legislation. The great tasks are no longer to be met except through endeavors that are organic and disciplinary. To this the anarchist temperament refuses to submit.

If the coöperative spirit triumph in the movement, it can come only through those inclinations that find their satisfaction in resolute team work. With competitive habits as old as the race struggle, this disposition to work helpfully together is created only as other habits are created. This is no more a moral test than it is an industrial test. By it Syndicalism as a constructive movement will stand or fall.

It may be doubted if any movement in existence is more calculated by its practical methods to defeat and to delay the coöperative temper and habit than

the I. W. W., as at present directed in the United
States. If there were some psychic scale or metre by
which we could measure the accumulation of anger
and resentment which sabotage alone kindles in the
heart of industrial managers, it would make a very
ghastly showing. I have never put this question to
one I. W. W. member who thought of this manufactured hostility except with satisfaction. The reply is,
"We want no coöperation with the employing class.
The less of it, the better and the more hope for us."
This does not meet the difficulty. It is not only that
the three-fold weapon of the I. W. W. enrages the
managers of business, *it angers and irritates a large part
of the wage earners.* At this moment the real strength of
Socialism and of trade unionism is against I. W. W.
methods. Much of the very best in these two bodies is
as hot in their protest as any capitalist manager.

Here, within the inner ranks of labor itself, the
I. W. W. creates the exact opposite of the coöperative
spirit and habit. As we have seen, these antagonisms
are already smarting among Syndicalists themselves.
This is the slippery anarchist slope from which the
movement will free itself with utmost difficulty. Its
raw fighting tactics are and have been its own worst
enemy, *if* and in so far as a coöperating commonwealth
is its declared hope.

This coöperative plan is nowhere better seen than
in the "Preferential shop" in New York garment
industries. The trade union, the employer and the
public have organic recognition. It is a form of co-
operation as educational to labor as it is to capital.
Automatically the consumer becomes a partner in

preserving the higher standards of income, conditions and sanitation.

Avoiding the perils of the "closed shop" collective bargaining and genuine labor organization are frankly recognized by employer and public alike. Even if, as syndicalists have it, capitalism is trembling on the edge of the abyss, the "protocol of peace" has an informing and educational influence so direct, so inclusive, so powerful that it should be welcomed by the rankest revolutionist as good preparatory discipline for those who are to reorganize the new society. That needs so rudimentary as these should be ignored is little to the credit of syndicalist campaigners.

The severest and most merited criticism of I. W. W. ways and means is: (1) their destructive character, and the consequent reaction on the habits of those who practice them; and (2) that these methods are treated as if they were principles of action: principles that can be safely entrusted in their application to miscellaneous masses of men and women in times of group excitement. It is not to such keeping that we shall entrust either our ethical or business destinies. If this means failure in all constructive achievement a question yet remains, What service if any, may we honestly assign to a movement dignified by such heroism and by inspiring sacrifices which lift it beyond our cynicism and beyond our moral indifference.

XVIII

THE SERVICE OF THE AWAKENER

In most of its present activities in the United States the I. W. W. is pretty exhaustively described by the word "Shocker." It startles the preoccupied by its new and unwonted approach. Like the stroke of a suffragette's hammer upon plate glass, it gets instant attention from every one within hearing.

I heard a man justify himself for personal rudeness on this ground: "I have a weak voice, and if I don't say disagreeable things, nobody will listen to me." The voice of the I. W. W. is not weak, but the society to which it speaks is deaf with a good deal of apathy and indifference. Only the very strident note will reach it. Every step toward larger justice or social protection seems possible only after some shock to the conscience or to the emotions.

We were deaf as adders to the truth about our city politics until a troop of muckrakers shouted the facts in our ears. We have at last begun to deal timidly with the "white slave traffic," though scarcely daring yet to put the deeper facts into words. Such depths of consenting hypocrisy have so long screened it from fearless investigation, that we cannot yet make a regulation that even touches the heart of it. Society has assented to it; found it "necessary" and then used prostitution to protect the virtue of favored classes until the evil has grown into the very structure and tissue of society. The stripped results are now frightening us into some sincerity. The Physician and Man of Science are now the shockers:—the Muckrakers in this new field. They are compelling us to look at some of the physical horrors which this evil inflicts by its cancerous reaction on the race.

As for its social origins and all its darker implications of social guilt and complicity, no one has ever put more needed truth than Bernard Shaw into a passage that most folk who think well of themselves should learn by heart. It concerns the recent attempt in England to pass a law for the flogging of certain persons engaged in this loathsome traffic. In the new organ, *The Awakener*, published by English women to deal with this evil (as we have started *Vigilance*) Mr. Shaw writes:

"And you, humble reader, who are neither a shareholder nor a landlord, do you thank God that you are guiltless in this matter? Take care! The first man flogged under the Act may turn on you and say, 'God shall smite thee, thou whited wall.' The wages of prostitution are stitched into your button-holes and into your blouse, pasted into your match-boxes and your boxes of pins, stuffed into your mattress, mixed with the paint on your walls, and stuck between the joints of your water-pipes. The very glaze on your basin and teacup has in it the lead poison that you offer to the decent woman as the reward of honest labor, whilst the procuress is offering chicken and champagne. Flog other people until you are black in the face and they are red in the back: You will not cheat the Recording Angel into putting down your debts to the wrong account."

It is not the jester who speaks in these words, it is the truthteller. Until the humbling lesson is learned by those addressed, all the gnawing miseries of this social disease will go on as of old.

This special evil is but one of many whose roots have reached such depths in our society that traditional palliatives, like many of our charities, do not even touch them. With all our enormous expenditure against crime, did it ever stalk among us with more effrontery in the United States than at the present moment?

It looks as if suffering or successive shocks alone could compel us to deal greatly and adequately with these evils. We do not even heed industrial and economic wrongs unless stunned and frightened into action. There were evils in Southern lumber camps quite unbelievable until I. W. W. "agitators" called attention to them.

But for these disturbers, we should apparently have looked on unconcerned while textile managers cut wages because the state had wisely lowered the working hours. A progressive social legislation should not be defeated by private decision in that manner. The consequences are far too serious for private determination. If a wage-cut which was so certain to involve social danger is necessary, it should at least have adequate public explanation. The end to these secret and absolute decisions, in which the public is intimately concerned, cannot come too soon. If I. W. W. tactics help to face these issues, their "agitators" then become educators and as such deserve approval.

In many other ways, they startle a too impassive

society into some sense of those darker realities in the midst of which we live partly in ignorance, partly by moral torpor.

It has long been half known that in many garish hotels and restaurants—the very ones to which "Easy Street" flocks for its jollities—that the conditions, the pay, and hours of work among certain of the lower serving class were inhumanly bad. For parts of this service, the vulgar briberies of the tipping system invited the abuse of uncertainty, envy, suspicion and exploitation. The weaker help especially among the women were worked far beyond legal limits. There was often an extremely vicious system of fining. Because of our inveterate social preoccupations these abuses might go on for decades. But suddenly from this underworld the smouldering heats burst into a "Waiters Strike." The thronged tables are unserved. Momentarily the fuss and clutter are great fun, except for the proprietors. These have spasms of choler which the public itself shares when the novelty is gone or the dinners too long delayed.

A specified list of complaints was given me at the meeting place of the cooks and waiters. I have submitted it to hotel managers and to stewards as well as to waiters in no way connected with the strike. These witnesses agree that some of the complaints are absurd; that some of the charges are groundless. They agree that much is demanded which is impossible to grant. They agree that the complaints do not apply to all hotels and restaurants. But they also agree in the only thing which concerns us, that very widely and where one should least expect it are utterly inexcusable abuses against the weaker and more obscure "help." An old steward with experience in many resorts put it—"these strikers are acting like lunatics but in a lot of the places where they work there is so much outrageous ill-treatment and so much besides which would disgust the public if they only knew about it, that any sort of an uproar if it brings out the facts is a good thing."

No investigator will ask more than that. Socially, we seem thus far to have developed no willingness or capacity to know about abuses or to acknowledge them, except through a catastrophe or the waste and noisy rumpus like that of a strike. These do definitely call attention to ignored evils. It required a devastating strike in England to show an astonished public that 100,000 men upon their railways were receiving scarcely one dollar a day—large numbers of them with families, and at a time when that dollar was shrinking to eighty cents because of rising prices. No one could be made to believe the miseries of the Pas-de-calais mines in the north of France until the long horrors of a strike compelled the public to look and to listen. It is the same dreary tale with our garment industries and with our textile mills down to the Lawrence strike. The Commissioner of Labor very calmly tells his story in a lengthy Report, and, because of the strike, people all over the country send greedy appeals for a copy. Hard by is Lowell made the object of a *Survey* under the auspices of a department of Harvard University. This study by one long resident in the city develops into a goodly book, without a bitter line from cover to cover. In

the spirit of good will, the author tries to spare that
most sensitive thing in the world—community pride,
but the truth comes out and is hungrily sought and
widely quoted because the drama at Lawrence had
startled the public. The volume has many passages
of which these are samples:— [1]

"One tenement had a record of six deaths in five
successive families in this tuberculosis incubator.
This showed the absolute necessity of protecting
people against themselves. It became necessary at
once to inspect the tenements, and the Board soon
found itself opposed by the greed of certain landlords.
Dirt, darkness and dampness, the three worst features
to fight, are fostered by such conditions. . . . One
landlord said in cold blood that property of this sort
had paid for itself within five years. But the price of
such a profit was the health of his tenants."

". . . the head nurse employed by the District
Nursing Department of the Middlesex Women's
Club, expressed herself forcibly upon the conditions
she found in her visits during the past year among
the sick poor. 'I have been amazed,' she said, 'literally stunned, by the conditions under which many
people live in Lowell. It is confined to no particular
locality; there are bad conditions, in spots, scattered
all over the city.'"

"Cellars are allowed to go unpurified by whitewash,
until the odor from them is discernible from the outside of the building. Then there are rotten timbers,
casements falling with decay, and a general atmosphere of dampness and mouldiness that is unwhole-

[1] *The Record of a City*, G. F. Kenngott; Macmillan & Co., 1912.

some. Moreover, the sanitary provisions are often in
wretched condition. Outside water-closets, sometimes windowless, connect with the houses; and for
purposes of practical economy, the owner of the
property occasionally has an arrangement by which
he attends to the flushing himself, once or twice a day,
as happens to be convenient. This keeps down the
water bill, but it can scarcely be expected to lower the
tenement house death-rate."

"The hapless condition of the unskilled labor is
apparent. Our earlier view is confirmed, that, when
the husband is the only wage-earner, he can rarely
support a wife and two small children. In his young
manhood, he and his little ones are in constant distress
from lack of nourishing food, clothing and simple
comforts. He is fairly comfortable for a few brief
years in middle life, when his children, between
fourteen and eighteen years of age, become wage-
earners and help to increase the family fund. Often,
when his earning capacity has diminished or ended,
he is found in a pitiable condition, with his family
scattered, and with nothing saved from his scanty
wages. All along the way he has met with accident,
sickness and unemployment caused by slack work,
shut-downs, strikes and lock-outs."

"The standard requirement of 400 cubic feet for
each adult for twenty-fours a day, exclusive of the
kitchen, is violated on every side in the congested
districts named."

"The largest wooden tenement blocks in 'Little
Canada,' 'The Harris,' has two shops and forty-eight
tenements of four rooms each, and often contains

about three hundred inhabitants. It has thirty rooms without windows."

Elementary sanitary protection is imperilled because "it is almost impossible for them to keep clean and healthy in the miserable, over-crowded tenements which they occupy here."

This far pulsing strike in a neighboring town makes men read this indictment. It opens the mind to evidence that otherwise would have no hearing. It is pitiful enough that such wrecking disturbances should be required even to make us look these evils in the face. But *until we learn a new solicitude for things that shame us, this sharp surgery of revolt is to be welcomed.*

It is directly to a threatening and rebuking Socialism that Europe owes much of its most effective social legislation. It literally scared society into some of its most elementary duties. Until we can act without threats, threats are our salvation—yes, even the threats of the I. W. W. This service they render, and it is not a mean one. They are telling plain truths to many sections of our community. They are challenging some of our old trade unions,—telling them of their lust for monopoly power: of their tendency to exclusiveness and snobbery toward the unskilled and less fortunate among the laborers. A trade union like some in the glass industry may develop every monopoly vice that capitalism shows at its worst. It may have the same hard complacency, the same indifference, the same need to be convicted of sin that is socially true of us all. I asked one of the oldest and best of our social settlement workers what, in order of demerit, was our chief sin. She said, "The sleep of

indifference among the comfortable, headed the
list."

The rebelling spirit of the I. W. W. is at least a
wholesome disquieter of this sleep. If we add to this,
its own awakening appeal to the more unfavored labor
in which its propaganda is carried on, we are merely
recognizing forces that are useful *until a wiser way is
found to do their work.* This we have not yet found,
neither have we greatly and searchingly tried to find
it. So many are our social inhumanities that the
rudest upsetting will do us good if the shock of it
forces us to our duties.

With much of the purposed *motive* of the I. W. W.
we may also sympathize. The goal at which they aim
is one from which every parasitic and unfair privilege
shall be cut out. I asked one of the best of them,
"What ultimately do you want?" "I want a world,"
he said, "in which every man shall get exactly what
he earns and *all* he earns;—a world in which no man
can live on the labor of another."

It is not conceivable that any rational person should
deny the justice and the reasonableness of that ideal.
Every step toward it is a step nearer a decent and more
self-respecting society. But progress toward those
larger equalities is very little helped by stating far off
ends. To play imaginatively with ideal perfections
is easy to the laziest of our faculties. We are, however,
not here in the sphere of poetry, but in the sphere of
suggested social reconstruction. Never till we reach
the question of means, measures, methods, is there the
slightest test of wisdom among those entering upon
tasks so formidable. Customs, institutions, and,

above all, the habits and thoughts of men have to be changed before one faltering step can be taken toward ultimate goals. Admitting that as shockers they do the hard, self-sacrificing work of necessary agitation and awakening, they bring no promise of constructive purpose. The heated energies of "direct action" should be held in real restraint by some great aim like that which coöperation offers. This "together-movement" is now permanently at home in several countries. It assumes many forms that offer immediate foothold for further growths. It is also a movement of future ideal promise, far more powerful to the imagination than all the mythical incantations of Mr. George Sorel.

If any man may be said to be the founder of Syndicalism, it is probably Fernand Pelloutier. He seems to have inspired profound respect in every man who knew him. He was first to show the real power of the united unions in getting things directly for themselves, rather than by appeal to shifty politicians, even of the socialist groups. His work was among the Labor Exchanges (Bourses du Travail),[1] some of which had, like their Italian brothers, tested coöperation. His faith and hope in the future of this "democratized industry" sustained him like a religion. Knowing well that his life was to be cut short by fatal disease, he worked with serene passion for the coming triumph of coöperation until the end. Now it is the supreme value of this ideal, that those who hold it are influenced in their choice of means and methods. If we

---

[1] His *Histoire des bourses du travail*, was published in Paris, in 1902.

are to be trained to work with each other, rather than
competitively against each other; if we are to substitute "democratic for aristocratic management;" if
labor groups are to assume the heavy risks of direction
as well as possible losses, then the one fatal thing is
not to educate labor for its coming duties. In the
light of this imperative need, all practices will be
tested. Strikes, boycott and sabotage will be curbed
and made severely incidental to something greater
than themselves. These negations will have no insane
and indiscriminate recommendation, as our I. W. W.
now give them in the United States. Positive virtues
will be kept at the front. From Pelloutier to Odon
Por this imperious necessity of training and education
seems to have been felt by a few leading spirits.

It is at this point that Sorel himself forgets his
"saving pessimism," his "Illusions of Progress" on
which he writes a book, his "Myths" and "fighting
virtues," for calm discussion of the possibilities of
coöperative credit in Raiffeisen banks that has freed
an army of small farmers from the clutch of the usurer.

As economic instructor, it is the one commanding
service of working coöperation, that it teaches labor
the functions of business. It not only brings out the
nature of market risks and the need of managers'
ability, but it puts every active member instantly to
school on the fundamental questions of property. No
profitable moment can be spent in discussing Socialism
apart from the nature and function of interest, rent
and profits.

Wherever Socialism has created its own coöperative
business in distribution, production, banking, it has

at once to deal practically with all these vital issues.

A coöperative village is quick to learn that all its inhabitants create their ground rent and *therefore* rent should go to their community and not to any speculating individual. They are as quick to learn that private interest on money is quite another matter. They learn that, at least under capitalism, it has its uses. They learn that if ever interest is to pass away, it cannot be until capital is far more widely diffused than now.

They learn to drop empty and barren formulas like "money cannot breed money" and face the plain fact. "Shall I lend my savings of 100 francs to the *Coöperative?* Our manager needs it and asks me for it. If I lend it to him to carry on the work of the store, I meantime cannot use it; neither can I get anything from it in the bank where I now get three per cent."

In exactly these terms, I have heard Belgian and Danish Socialists talk about interest. They learned thus intimately to face one of the great questions on which the future of Socialism will turn. Even if interest and profits are now necessary evils under the perversions of capitalism—can they be altogether dispensed with under Socialism? Or will interest and profits, stripped of present abuses, still have such utilities in so stimulating savings as to justify their continued use, even when the monopolies have been socialized? That Syndicalism at its highest should have recognized an ideal so admirable puts it safely beyond cheap and sniffy criticism. That such ideal should have developed where the movement is oldest, may warrant the hope that time and experience may give it sanity elsewhere.

This, however, raises an awkward difficulty. Syndicalism is in no way distinguished from other movements by this ideal expression of the coöperative brotherhood. At whatever point its main energies pass into constructive coöperation, it is at one with many other daring hopes and efforts that for two generations have looked toward the "democratizing of life and opportunity by democratizing industry." Let it be said again, there is no proper or final estimate of any new social movement by the ideal end it sets before us. Far more is it to be judged by its practical and intermediate measures. It is these chiefly that set Syndicalism apart from others in the field and by these is it mainly to be judged.

I listened in Seattle to an orator in the street flaying capitalism and trade unions with an impartial lash. When he stepped panting from his perch, I asked him what he was really after in the special strike for which he was pleading. "What are we after? Why, we are after that mill. We have made it and every machine in it. It is a product of our labor and it belongs to us."

As if driving spikes, he had told his audience how this was to be brought about. He made no mystery of "direct action" and sabotage. To and fro among the crowd men passed, selling literature in which these measures were set forth with authoritative detail, quite in the manner of the orator.

To my suggestion that deep behind the mill in question were centuries of socially sanctioned forms of property—that plans, organization, purchase of machinery, creating a market, with all the risks involved, and that these also were a part of his problem, —the only answer I could get was that they were not engaged in splitting hairs. "Capitalism," he said, "has us by the throat, and we shall act accordingly." It is wholly safe to say that no body of workingmen in the world, who for two years had achieved even modest success in productive-coöperation, would have seen so little of the real problem or attempted its solution by methods that, for the most part, merely wasted hard-earned wealth created by employer, boss, and "labor" alike.

XIX

SOME DUTIES OF OUR OWN

It is true that the I. W. W. can have stable relations
neither with the socialist party nor with existing trade
unionism. In tumultuous days like those at Lawrence,
when labor and capital are at each other's throats,
Socialist and Syndicalist will join hands. Money will
pour in from the general public, including every class,
"idle rich," "intellectuals," and even from active
business men far removed from local heats and bias.
This miscellaneous response may carry no imaginable
approval of I. W. W. tenets or practices. It may be
solely from the conviction that local employers and
public authorities are using their strength in bad
temper or brutally and unjustly against the labor side
in the fight. I have pointed to the growth of this
vague but powerful sympathy as a new factor no
longer to be ignored. If it reach a certain pitch,
nothing can keep it out of politics and from the uses
to which politicians will put it. Socialist party members will help the I. W. W. at the points of contest
precisely as this general public did at Lawrence, but
in every month that passes, the logic of all that is
clearly distinctive of the I. W. W. will show a deepen-
ing gulf between them and all Socialism based upon
and committed to political action. W. D. Haywood
is now on the National Executive Board of the
socialist party. There is as little intellectual consist-

ency, either for him or for the party, that he should
be there, as that he should be in the Republican
Party or the Catholic church. This is not to defame
him, but to define him. He is as much out of place on
that Board as an orthodox Single Taxer. In his
writings and speeches, he represents with extraor-
dinary fidelity the primitive, undisciplined forces in
Syndicalism. With epigrammatic skill, he voices this
fast emerging and plaintive aspiration which lowlier
and ignored masses of working men and women are
coming to feel; those without votes; those that no
trade union would have for the asking; those who can
be shoved aside and "put upon" because they neither
speak our tongue nor know our ways—these half be-
wildered legions become articulate in this agitator
who is to that extent educator. They recognize something in him which feeds hungers that in some way
have to be fed. It is a craving which no church,
catholic or protestant, can satisfy. Its urgency is
untouched by religious appeal because the heart of it
is economic. No delayed other-worldly appeal will
divert it.

The speech or symbol that can reach and rouse
them is not meanly to be thought of, nor should any
pharisaical arrogance set such an one wholly at naught.
It is because this heart of reality is in the movement
as a whole, that our problem with the I. W. W. is so
beset by perplexities. There is much in its motive to
command our respect. In its active striving, there is
much with which society will have to coöperate or
suffer from its lack of intelligent sympathy. The
proletariat, the "fourth estate," or by whatever name

we call it, has in some way to be brought nearer to the sources of economic security. The insistence that this should be done and the belief in its possibilities, if society will use the resources at its disposal, have now become a great and passionate faith. Every higher spiritual movement in the politics and religion of our time reflects this faith. It is a service so great and so difficult that no one who can help it is to be outlawed.

For example, we shall never take one enlightened step in reconstructing the futilities of present criminal procedure, until we learn to coöperate in a new spirit with those who have suffered inside the prison. No man on the outside is good enough or wise enough to "represent" them. They should have their own representatives to instruct and guide us by that experience which no outsider ever knows because he has not lived it.

As little do people, economically secure, know the life of the "fourth estate." Our pretence to know it makes our ignorance the more dangerous. These used and ignored masses should also have their own representatives. All attempts to prevent this are now too late. Very imperfectly, but with its own invincible reality, the syndicalist stirring in the world speaks for the weak and neglected many. This part of the message we must understand. We must "recognize" it, as those eager and willing to coöperate with every climbing desire to equalize opportunity in the world. In no other way shall we either teach ourselves or carry help to those who need it.

It can be most confidently set down, that with the whole list of social "remedies"—profit sharing, arbitration, "welfare work" in all its varieties,—the abiding successes will depend upon the degree and intelligent heartiness with which the representatives of labor are encouraged to coöperate with business management. An authoritative and one-sided ascendency in these things was once possible and in spots may be so still, but their day, for much of our industry, is gone and soon will end for the whole of it. In thirty years we have seen scores of these fine schemes wrecked because of lurking insincerity in the proclaimed objects.

In the larger and more general field of social contact and discussion, it is as clumsily fatal to act in the old absolutist spirit, as to attempt railway management in the "public-be-damned" manner of the earlier magnates of transportation. The old feeling may still be there but it can neither be publicly expressed nor successfully acted upon. They have now to coöperate with government and every day will be forced into completer coöperation. In many countries not a step can now be taken in most social legislation without the assenting coöperation with Socialism.

No considerable force appearing among us seeking social betterment is to be held off and treated like a marauder or an outcast. Invariably these forces bring with them idealisms that no society can afford to lose. Much of the conscious plan and method of Syndicalism is whimsically chimerical. But in it and through it is something as sacred as the best of the great dreamers have ever brought us. In the total of this movement, the deeper, inner fact seems to me to be its nearness to and sympathy with that most heavy laden and long enduring mass of common toilers. Alike to our peril and to our loss, shall we ignore this fact. Steadily to see it and keep it in remembrance is the beginning of such practical wisdom as we may show toward it.

In large numbers, especially in the rank and file, are those who, through some experience, have really wakened to the tragic ugliness of poverty and insecurity.

In the actual facts of working Syndicalism in our very midst, the idea *as motive* may be seen in any overwrought community where the I. W. W. holds sway. Deeply to convince any ardent and generous nature that our own capitalistic "law and order" is desperately and hopelessly corrupt: that it condemns day by day multitudes of guiltless workers to a life degrading to the individual and perilous to the family, and that their condition steadily grows worse, is in itself an appeal to heroic virtues. What is one utterly gone over to this belief to do? What steps are wise advisers to take with such as these? Several times personally, I have had to face this: once with a lad of twenty who had given himself with complete and tremulous devotion to a cause that seemed to him more sacred than any religion of which he knew. He was moved by an emotion so clean and intense that death on a barricade would have frightened him as little as a girl's smile. Awkwardly, and with stuttering apologies, I could only try to prove how and why I thought he was mistaken. It was easy to see while I talked, that he was listening to other voices that he respected more, and more gladly heard. It was like telling a young twelfth century Crusader, fired and panting for departure, that he was imprudent, that the facts were all against him, that he was spoiling a career, that the holy sepulchre was not after all in any real peril. A young college woman told me that the "new movement" came to her like a great light; that it had given her such a peace in her heart as she had never known. "All that I can give and become," she said, "goes to discredit a society in which one cannot ever have self-respect." Young Christians doubtless spoke like that when to be known as Christian was to be marked for torture. In very considerable numbers, the like of these are there in our I. W. W. crusade. They are practically inseparable from those with coarser ignorances and meaner motives. Unless these idealisms are held rather tenderly in mind, we shall neither see nor estimate the larger movement with either truth, justice, or safety to ourselves.

At the risk of weariness to the reader, it must be repeated that present labor troubles differ from those in the past chiefly in this, that they now develop in a new and changed atmosphere. They attract a wider and more powerful public sympathy which enables the politician to play in them a new and more effective rôle. It does not help us to throw the blame upon the politician, or would-be politician. Every whit of his strength is in the public opinion that he merely reflects. No politician who took a hand in the recent strike on the Boston Elevated had an atom of real influence except what general opinion gave him.

If this had been recognized, many a public service corporation would have been spared humiliation.

A dozen towns have been amazed and indignant that they must submit to a prying invasion from the Government, from politicians, and an army of outside investigators. This enlargement and intensifying of popular sympathy is the first capital fact which no wise employer or owner will in future ignore. The spread of this sympathy will compel business management in all conspicuous business to revalue the whole *human* side of its problem. I do not mean that it should be friendlier or more philanthropic. I mean that the fatal note of arbitrariness and priggish aloofness has got to go. Labor, with its powers of collective bargaining, must be met in a spirit that is strictly coöperative—coöperative in the sense of some recognized equality between the status of labor and that of capital. Business must put as high ability into the human side as into the financial. It has got to drop a good deal of its pride, secrecy, and airs of superiority.

Whether it has to face the trade union, the Socialists, or the more revolutionary I. W. W., they must one and all be met naturally and, above all, humanly. In the strict sense, they have got to be "recognized" and openly dealt with for the sole reason that the human side of business can in no other way be wisely dealt with.

In all that I have been able to ascertain about outbreaks in thirteen Eastern and Western communities, the I. W. W. got its grip where trade unionism had been beaten, or had no existence, or had been so weakened as to offer little resistance. Trade unions as powerful as those in Germany, where they are in closest sympathetic touch with a disciplined socialism, leave syndicalism without a foothold, except for a few harmless eccentrics.

In France many of the unions are notoriously so unstable and unbuttressed by funds as to give every advantage to syndicalist experiments. To hold office in a "pure and simple" trade union, is to be excluded from I. W. W. membership. There are no editors admitted except those on their own journals. Though their entire conception is based upon trained skill within the shops and everywhere "at the point of production," they glory in their appeal to the unskilled—to those hitherto unreached by labor associations.

But a few months after their first convention in 1905, they attacked the hotels and restaurants in Goldfield, Nevada, In rapid succession follow Youngstown, Ohio; Portland, Oregon; and again Goldfield in 1907, where they claim to have secured eight hours and $4.50 per day. We have throughout the same story of enfeebled unionism or none at all. If the American Federation has some partial hold, that of itself brings war with the I. W. W., as at Skowhegan Mills in 1907, Youngstown and Bridgeport. To the I. W. W. any unionist of the American Federation of Labor is a scab and an outlaw.

In the desperate eleven weeks' strike in 1909 at McKees Rocks, Pa., unionism had been crippled.[1]

[1] It was at this strike that the I. W. W. met the most efficient State Constabulary yet evolved in the States. Between seven and eight thousand men with 14 or 15 nationalities met this body. On the killing of the first striker, the war was on. The General Secretary of the I. W. W. thus comments on it:

At Lawrence, by express purpose, unionism had been stifled. "This was great luck for us," as one expressed it. "Gompers' fakirs had been kept out and we had our chance."

New Bedford followed. I met one hurrying to this new field. "We will put New Bedford on the map, too," he said. But it did not then get on to the map. With bad generalship, the invaders fell upon a mill long organized. These men felt so competent to manage their own affairs that the failure of the I. W. W. was immediate and complete.

There is but one fair inference from this wide experience. If capitalist management, itself endowed with every advantage of organization, deliberately refuses it to labor, capital will suffer. It will suffer because public opinion and the political action which that opinion reflects, will more and more take sides with labor in every struggle that becomes conspicuous. This wider public will side even with turbulent and disorganized masses like the I. W. W. It will be said, and justly said, "The fight is too grossly unfair." The public will say this and act upon it, in spite of all

"The strike committee then served notice upon the commander of the cossacks that for every striker killed or injured by the cossacks the life of a cossack would be exacted in return. And that they were not at all concerned as to which cossack paid the penalty, but that a life for a life would be exacted. The strikers kept their word. On the next assault by the cossacks, several of the constabulary were killed and a number wounded. The cossacks were driven from the streets and into the plants of the company. An equal number of strikers were killed and about 50 wounded in the battle. This ended the killing on both sides during the remainder of the strike. For the first time in their existence the cossacks were 'tamed.' The McKees Rocks strike resulted in a complete victory for the strikers."

atrocities by McNamaras caught and uncaught. It will so act because it has learned that point for point, capital has its own ugly record of lawless misdemeanor that is at least as threatening to social peace and welfare as all the ill-bred violence of labor.

Such resources has great capital, that it has been able to cloak its evil doing in veiled, legal decencies, while labor must go to its sinning naked and exposed. This too the public has learned. It has learned it so well that conspicuous business can no longer act in the spirit of "I'll manage my business as I like." This public has also come to feel that all the gilded welfare schemes which only screen secret and arbitrary power over labor have probably had their day. The great and healing resources left us are those of "social insurance," meant primarily to secure labor against those dire fatalities—sickness, accident, unemployment, and death. The best of them are far more generous and more efficient for those insured than any government insurance in the world. They are open to the freest investigation by every employee. Whether capitalism has yet a long life or a short one, these private schemes are of very highest value. They are educating the race in the great art of self-protection. If Socialism were to come to-morrow, it would use these institutions as models. With all their excellence, there is one drawback. More and more labor suspects them. As they depend utterly upon the willing coöperation of labor, this gangrene of suspicion sets too narrow limits to their widest efficiency as "remedies."

We are thus driven to one further step. This can have no statement except as a general principle, but it is one in the light of which every special welfare plan may be safely tested. It is this—In these larger concerns wage earners from now on must be made to understand that the business is *in some sense* theirs; that they shall have their own genuine representation in the management. The beginnings will be very modest, but they must be so open and free from dissembling, as to give labor faith enough to warrant its own coöperation. It is because these beginnings must be so modest, that the door should be fearlessly open to as much increased labor representation as results justify.

This principle of a progressive participation of labor in management, forces the frankest "recognition" that every party concerned must be taken (through its representatives) into the inner councils. This involves a publicity of business method and conditions which labor and the public now demand. The suspicions of the public are nearly as aggressive as those of labor. Not a month passes that this suspicion does not deepen.

The most impelling purpose in the movement called Syndicalism is its powerful, half-blind urgency toward the democratizing of economic power in the world. From now on politics will more and more be used to this end. As the old enemies, Democrat and Republican, in Milwaukee fall into each other's arms in order to drive Socialists from the City Hall, we shall elsewhere see the larger interests of property oblivious of old party lines, uniting in their defense against the general socialist encroachment. This encroachment is impulsive: it is not sagacious but it rises higher and

higher among the people against the whole inner
kingdom of hedged and secret privilege, out of which
inequalities spring which rational men no longer
justify. There will be infinite variation of opinion as
to ways and means through which these too absolute
economic powers are to be brought under social control. That in some way this has to be done, few men
of detached and disinterested intelligence any longer
doubt. To do this work legally and in the spirit of a
social legislation which at last enrolls in its service
the very best that science, education and a cleaner
politics have to offer, is the ennobling hope now
before us.

Within a quarter of a century in a dozen countries,
the actual work in establishing new and permanent
standards of health, education and opportunity are
the supreme achievements of our time, because they
lie at the foundation of any and every attempt at
social reconstruction which has the slightest promise
of performing that hardest of all tasks—democratizing
economic power and privilege. Of the time required
for this task; of the difficulties involved; of the long
educational and disciplinary needs, the wisest among
us have but shadowy knowledge.

As for constructive suggestion, our I. W. W. have
so little as to embarrass the most indulgent critic.
In their convulsive and incendiary appeal to the forgotten masses, there is, nevertheless, a saving utility
that should bring the movement within our sympathetic acceptance. To the utmost, we should work
with it as those determined to learn, from whatever
source the message come.

Of this total rising protest against sources of unnatural inequalities in wealth and opportunity, the I. W. W. is at most a very tiny part. It is yet enough that they are in it, and that they are fully aware of the fact. For the first time they are so consciously related to this spirit of revolt and to the delicate industrial mechanism which gives them power, that only a captious temper will refuse them hearing. Not by any churlish aloofness are they to be educated, nor are we ourselves to be educated. In all our efforts to penetrate these mysteries of social reformation, a common darkness is over us all.

Not in the least are those who most materially profit by the present system to be held in awe as possessors of special and exclusive enlightenment. There is also a "wisdom of the humble" endowed with the high authority of age-long suffering and experience. It is even to such as these that a new power is now passing. It will not be taken from them. It will be used in folly and cruelty, if society is also foolish and cruel.

It is the final condemnation of the old lone-hand, fighting spirit in industry, that it at once creates new and deadlier sources of antagonism. It revives on the spot, not public, but private warfare, with all its contagious treacheries.

The sole cure for these barbaric survivals is the coöperative intention developed into habits of thought and action. This intention need no longer expend itself in vague benevolence. New organs are at hand in which it may be embodied.

If we add to this the final best step of all—the open, declared purpose to admit labor to management first at safe and possible points with all that this means of banished secrets; to admit it fearlessly and with no reserves as far as labor proves its fitness; we then and there connect ourselves with the coöperative régime. This does not close the fist, it opens the arms. It is the essence of this coöperative intention—not to exclude, but to include labor in the control of business; courageously to give it every opportunity of training to this end. It will require the severe schooling of a century—but every strong man who openly sets his face that way, who tries consentingly and forbearingly to prove the policy wise is the helper to whom we look.

With this spirit and purpose we merely meet Syndicalism at its highest and best, rather than at its lowest and worst. At its ideal level, we take it at its own word. This ideal is also coöperation with the long educational drill which that implies. To unite with that ideal, to bear with the defeats incident to its slow unfolding, is to work securely with order and progress, and not against them. It is to work as securely with the ever wider and more intelligent good will of every class and condition of men on which the stability of social welfare must forever depend.

LITERATURE

There is no attempt to give here anything like a complete bibliography. The books, pamphlets and leaflets are those which the writer has found most useful in this study. The full report of the Chicago Convention (1905) has great value to the student and may be had, I think, through publishing centers here indicated.

American Literature

The volume referred to in the text by Mr. W. E. Walling, "Socialism As It Is," Macmillan & Co., shows analytical power in stating the issues from the more revolutionary point of view which gives it real importance in the study of syndicalism.

Dr. Louis Levine's "Labor Movement in France," Longmans, Green & Co., 1912, is admirable in its impartiality.

Pamphlets

"The I. W. W.; Its History, Structure and Methods," Vincent St. John. Price 10 cents.

"Why Strikes Are Lost; How to Win," Wm. E. Trautmann. Price 5 cents.

"The Farm Laborer and the City Worker," Edward McDonald. Price 5 cents.

Leaflets

"Political Parties and the I. W. W.," Vincent St. John.

"Getting Recognition," A. M. Stirton.

"Two Kinds of Unionism," Edward Hammond.

"Appeal to Wage Workers, Men and Women," E. S. Nelson.

"Union Scabs and Others," Oscar Ameringer.

"War and the Workers," Walker C. Smith.

"Address to Railroad Graders," "Rusty" Mitchell.

"The Tramp As a Homeguard," Jean E. Spielman.

"Why the A. F. of L. Cannot Become an Industrial Union," Vincent St. John.

Each of above leaflets, 15 cents per hundred; $1.25 per thousand. I. W. W. Publishing Bureau, P. O. Box 622, New Castle, Pa.

"On the Firing Line," published by The Industrial Worker, P. O. Box 2129, Spokane, Washington.

"One Big Union," Trautmann.

"Direct Action and Sabotage," Trautmann.

"Industrial Union Methods," Trautmann.

"Industrial Socialism," Haywood & Bohn.

"General Strike," Haywood.

"Proletarian and Petit Bourgeois," Austin Lewis.

"Militant Proletariat," Lewis.

"Rise of the American Proletarian."

Published by Socialist News Co., 342 Third Ave., Pittsburg, Pa.

The Three I. W. W. papers (in English) are "The Industrial Worker," (weekly) $1.00 per year. P. O. Box 2129, Spokane, Washington.

"Solidarity," (weekly) $1.00. P. O. Box 622, New Castle, Pa.

By the "Detroit Branch," "The Industrial Union News," (monthly) 50 cents. 96 Brush St., Detroit, Mich.

"The International Socialist Review," (monthly) $1.00. C. H. Kerr & Co., 118 Kinzie St., Chicago, is indispensable in following the movement in this country. W. D. Haywood is an associate editor and frequent contributor.

I. W. W. Song Books

To Fan the Flames of Discontent:

"Songs of Joy!"

"Songs of Sorrow!"

"Songs of Sarcasm!"

"Songs of the Miseries That Are."

"Songs of the Happiness To Be."

May be had, P. O. Box 622, New Castle, Pa.

English

"Syndicalism and the General Strike," Arthur D. Lewis.
309 pp. Publisher, T. Fisher Unwin, London, 1912.
"Syndicalism," J. H. Harley, M. A. Publisher, T. C. & E. C.
Jack, London.
"Syndicalism and Labour," Sir Arthur Clay. 230 pp. Pub-
lisher, E. P. Dutton and Company, New York, 1911.
"The Worker and His Country," Fabian Ware. 288 pp. Pub-
lisher, Edward Arnold, London, 1912. The author shows
strong sympathy with the syndicalists, and has intimate
knowledge of the French movement.
"The Miner's Next Step." Robert Davies & Company,
London, 1912.
"Industrial Unionism and the Mining Industry," George
Harvey. Published by Socialist Labour Party, 28 Forth
St., Edinboro.
"Syndicalism," J. Ramsay MacDonald. Publisher, Constable,
London, 1912.
"The Philosopher of Change," Henri Bergson. Publisher
W. Carr, 67 Long Ave., London.
This useful little volume of 90 pp. is in "The People's Books"
series.

French

"Le Syndicalisme Contemporain," A. Zévaès. 22 Rue Huy-
ghens, Paris, 1911. An elaborate study of 358 pp., es-
pecially valuable from Chapter V–XI.
"Syndicalisme et Socialisme," Hubert Lagardelle, Arturo
Labriola and others. Marcel Rivière, 30 Rue Jacob, Paris.
"Histoire des bourses du travail," F. Pelloutier. Paris, 1902.
"Le Sabotage," E. Pouget. Paris, 1910.
"Les bases du Syndicalisme," E. Pouget. Paris.
"Syndicalisme révolutionnaire et Syndicalisme réformiste,"
Félicien Challaye. Paris, Alcan, 1909.
"Anarchisme individualiste," Edward Berth.
"Comment nous ferons la Révolution," E. Pataud et E. Pouget.

"A. B. C. Syndicaliste," Georges Yvetot. 3 Rue de Pondichéry, 1908.

"La Confédération Générale du Travail,'' Émile Pouget. Marcel Rivière, 30 Rue Jacob, Paris.

"L'Action Syndicaliste," Victor Griffuelhes. Marcel Rivière, 30 Rue Jacob, Paris.

"La Décomposition du Marxisme," and "Les Illusions du progres," 2d ed., 1911, Georges Sorel. Marcel Rivière, 30 Rue Jacob, Paris.

"Réflexions sur la Violence," Georges Sorel. Publisher, Marcel Rivière, 30 Rue Jacob, Paris.

"Les Syndicats et la Révolution," L. Niels. 140 Rue Mouffetard, Paris, 1902.

"La Philosophie Syndicaliste," Guy-Grand. 2d ed., Paris, 1911.

German

"Der moderne französische Syndikalismus," Dr. Anton Acht. Verlag von Gustav Fischer, Jena, 1911.
A severely academic study, but one of the most useful yet published.

The voluminous Italian literature I have not seen except such as appears in French translations. Something of this will be found in the French sources noted above.

INDEX

A

Absolutism, the democratic rising against capitalistic, 46.

Adulteration of foods, 132–134.

Agreements in garment-makers' strike, New York, attacked by I. W. W., 89 n.

Agriculture, coöperative work in, in Italy, 199–200.

American Federation of Labor, the, 53, 68–69, 72; members of, held as scabs by I. W. W., 246.

American Railway Union strike (1894), 104.

Amsterdam dockers' strike (1903), 124.

Anarchism, the I. W. W. and, 30, 168 ff.; strength of tendencies toward, in American Syndicalism, 172; French Syndicalists who believe in, 172; element of, peculiar to the I. W. W., 175; in Italy, 176–178.

Anarchy during strikes, 78.

Angel, Norman, *The Great Illusion* by, 116 n.

Antagonisms, class, 106–114.

Anthracite Coal Commission, 29.

Apart colonies, 51.

Arbitration, 52, 242.

Arbitration acts, rejection of Canadian, by I. W. W., 147.

Atlantic Monthly, 10.

Australian ballot, disappointment in scope of results from, 51.

Australian strike of 1890, 124 n.

Awakener, service of the I. W. W. as an, 225–238.

Awakener, The, English magazine, 226.

B

Bax, Belfort, opposition of, to sabotage, 153.

Bergson, Henri, 99; as "the philosopher of the unutterable," 169 n.

Bernstein, E., *Der Politische Massenstreik* by, 126 n.; committed to compensation, 183.

Berth, Edouard, 99; sabotage opposed by, 153; anarchist protest of, 171.

Bohn, Frank, quoted concerning the thirty-three dynamiters, 162.

Bonus systems, 52.

Boston Elevated Railroad strike, 23, 244.

Bourget, Paul, on Sorel, 172.

Boycott, perils of the, 70, 71.

Brewery workers, rejection of Old Age Pension offer by, 54–55.

Briand, 98.

Bryce, James, 48.

Burke, Edmund, quoted, 36.

Burns, John, 98.

to, 9, 117, 131; trial of, as viewed by French syndicalist reporter, 91; quoted on violence in the code of the I. W. W., 159.

F

Faure, Syndicalist veteran, 137.
Favre, Jules, 115.
Fourier, 47, 65, 141.
France, socialism in, 3; Haywood's account of the general strike in, 117–118; reformist parties in, 221–222; advantage to syndicalist experiments in, from weakness of trade unions, 246.

G

Garibaldi's army, an illustration from, 22.
Garment-makers' strike, New York, 89 n.
General Confederation of Labor, 75.
General strike, the, 71, 86–87, 93, 115–128.
Germany, Socialism in, 3; weakness of Syndicalism in, due to strength of labor unions, 245–246.
Ghent, W. J., on socialism in the Roosevelt programme, 100; on the class war, 108; on sabotage, 154.
Giovannitti, trial of, 8 n.; mentioned, 9.
Girardin, E. de, 115.
Goldfield, Nevada, I. W. W. attacks in, 246.

Gompers, 79.
Government interference in industrial affairs, 28–29; influence of public opinion upon, 31.
Grand Lodge, the, of the Owenites, 61, 62.
Grand National Consolidated Trade Unions of 1834, 93.
"Gréviculture," 135.
Griffuehles, Victor, L'Action Syndicaliste by, 123 n.; quoted, 128, 131; mentioned, 135 n.
Guèsde, 153.
Guild life of Middle Ages, strikes in the, 116

H

Hardy, Keir, 153.
Harley, J. H., Syndicalism by, 63 n.
Haywood, William D., 69, 82, 85, 91, 178; a production of the Colorado miners' strike, 75–77; Industrial Socialism by, quoted, 80; The General Strike by, quoted, 117–120; lack of consistency in position of, on National Executive Board of socialist party, 239–240.
Henderson, C. H., Pay-Day by, quoted, 187–188.
Hillquit, Morris, quoted on compensation, 186.
Homestead strike, 13.
Hugo, Victor, 115.
Humbert, King, murder of, 176–177.
Hunter, Robert, quoted, 154 n.